Passing Assessments for the Certificate in Education and Training

Ann Gravells and Susan Simpson

Los Angeles | London | New Delhi
Singapore | Washington DC

Learning Matters
An imprint of SAGE Publications Ltd
1 Oliver's Yard
55 City Road
London EC1Y 1SP

SAGE Publications Inc.
2455 Teller Road
Thousand Oaks, California 91320

SAGE Publications India Pvt Ltd
B 1/1 1 Mohan Cooperative Industrial Area
Mathura Road
New Delhi 110 044

SAGE Publications Asia-Pacific Pte Ltd
3 Church Street
#10–04 Samsung Hub
Singapore 049483

Editor: Amy Thornton
Development editor: Jennifer Clark
Production controller: Chris Marke
Project management: Deer Park Productions,
    Tavistock, Devon, England
Marketing Manager: Catherine Slinn
Cover design: Wendy Scott
Typeset by: C&M Digitals (P) Ltd, Chennai, India
Printed by Henry Ling Limited at The Dorset Press,
    Dorchester, DT1 1HD

Library of Congress Control Number: 2014930441

British Library Cataloguing in Publication data

A catalogue record for this book is available from the
British Library.

MIX
Paper from
responsible sources
FSC
www.fsc.org   FSC™ C013985

ISBN: 978-1-4462-9593-9 (pbk)
ISBN: 978-1-4462-9594-6

CONTENTS

Acknowledgements   vii
Author statements   viii

Introduction   1

    The structure of the book and how to use it   1
    Self-assessment activities and guidance for evidencing achievement   2
    The Certificate in Education and Training   3
    Assessment methods and activities   7
    Referencing work   12
    Study skills and reflective practice   14

Unit: Understanding roles, responsibilities and relationships in education and training

  1 Understand the teaching role and responsibilities in education and training   19

  2 Understand ways to maintain a safe and supportive learning environment   28

  3 Understand the relationships between teachers and other professionals
in education and training   34

Unit: Planning to meet the needs of learners in education and training

  4 Be able to use initial and diagnostic assessment to agree individual
learning goals with learners   41

  5 Be able to plan inclusive teaching and learning in accordance with
internal and external requirements   49

  6 Be able to implement the minimum core in planning inclusive
teaching and learning   59

  7 Be able to evaluate own practice when planning inclusive
teaching and learning   66

Unit: Delivering education and training

  8 Be able to use inclusive teaching and learning approaches in
accordance with internal and external requirements   74

9   Be able to communicate with learners and other learning
    professionals to promote learning and progression   81

10 Be able to use technologies in delivering inclusive
    teaching and learning   89

11 Be able to implement the minimum core when delivering inclusive
    teaching and learning   95

12 Be able to evaluate own practice in delivering inclusive
    teaching and learning   101

Unit: Assessing learners in education and training

13 Be able to use types and methods of assessment to meet the needs
    of individual learners   108

14 Be able to carry out assessments in accordance with internal and
    external requirements   119

15 Be able to implement the minimum core when assessing learners   126

16 Be able to evaluate own assessment practice   131

Unit: Using resources for education and training

17 Be able to use resources in the delivery of inclusive
    teaching and learning   137

18 Be able to implement the minimum core when using resources
    in the delivery of inclusive teaching and learning   146

19 Be able to evaluate own use of resources in the delivery of inclusive
    teaching and learning   152

20 **Teaching practice**   160

    Teaching practice   160
    Observed practice   162
    Ofsted criteria and grading characteristics   166
    The minimum core   170

Appendix   Qualification structure for the Level 4 Certificate in
           Education and Training   174

Index   176

ACKNOWLEDGEMENTS

The authors would like to give special thanks to the following people who have helped and contributed towards this book. They have freely given their time, knowledge and advice, resulting in some excellent contributions:

Dawn Upton

Lindsay Simpson

Vic Grayson

Special thanks go to both authors' family members for their patience and support, and to readers of the previous edition for their valuable feedback.

The authors would like to thank their editor Jennifer Clark for her continued support and excellent guidance.

Special thanks go to Amy Thornton from Learning Matters (which is part of SAGE Publications Ltd) for her advice, encouragement and tremendous patience with all our questions, emails and telephone calls.

Every effort has been made to trace the copyright holders and to obtain their permission for the use of copyright material. The publisher and authors will gladly receive any information enabling them to rectify any error or omission in subsequent editions.

Ann Gravells

Susan Simpson

AUTHOR STATEMENTS

Ann Gravells

Ann is a director of her own company Ann Gravells Ltd, an educational consultancy based in East Yorkshire. She specialises in teaching, training, assessment and quality assurance for the Further Education and Skills Sector.

Ann creates resources for teachers and learners such as PowerPoints and handouts for teaching and assessment qualifications. These are available via her resource website (www. anngravells.co.uk/resources).

Ann is a consultant to the University of Cambridge's Institute of Continuing Education. She has worked for several awarding organisations producing qualification guidance, policies and procedures, and carrying out quality assurance of teacher training qualifications. She has been teaching in further education colleges since 1983.

Ann holds a Master's in Educational Management, a PGCE, a Degree in Education, and a City & Guilds Medal of Excellence for teaching. Ann is a Fellow of the Institute for Learning and holds QTLS status.

She is often asked how her surname should be pronounced. The 'vells' part of Gravells is pronounced like 'bells'.

She is the author of:

Delivering Employability Skills in the Lifelong Learning Sector (2010)

Principles and Practice of Assessment in the Lifelong Learning Sector (2011)

Passing PTLLS Assessments (2012)

Preparing to Teach in the Lifelong Learning Sector (2012)

What is Teaching in the Lifelong Learning Sector? (2012)

Passing Assessments for the Award in Education and Training (2013)

The Award in Education and Training (2014)

Achieving your Assessor and Quality Assurance Units (2014)

She has edited:

Study Skills for PTLLS (2012)

Susan Simpson

Susan Simpson specialises in teaching, training, assessment and quality assurance for the Further Education and Skills Sector. She has been teaching since 1980.

Susan is the Lead for Communities and Partnerships for North East Lincolnshire Council. Susan was previously the Head of Community Learning Services, and has worked as a curriculum manager for Education and Training, ICT, Business Administration and Law. She developed, managed and taught adult education programmes in Botswana for 10 years. Susan has also presented at regional level for teacher training and nationally for ICT Skills for Life.

Susan holds a Post-graduate Diploma in Management Studies, BA (Hons) in Further Education and Training, and a Certificate in Education (Hons) in Business Studies and Economics.

Ann and Susan have co-authored:

Planning and Enabling Learning in the Lifelong Learning Sector (2010)

Passing CTLLS Assessments (2011)

Equality and Diversity in the Lifelong Learning Sector (2012)

The Certificate in Education and Training (2014)

Passing Assessments for the Certificate in Education and Training (2014)

Ann and Susan welcome any comments from readers; please contact them via Ann's website (www.anngravells.co.uk).

In this chapter you will learn about:

- the structure of the book and how to use it
- self-assessment activities and guidance for evidencing achievement
- the Certificate in Education and Training
- assessment methods and activities
- referencing work
- study skills and reflective practice.

The structure of the book and how to use it

This book is designed to help you assess the skills and knowledge you already have, in preparation for your formal assessments towards the Certificate in Education and Training. It is not a textbook, but a self-assessment book, and should therefore be read in conjunction with an appropriate textbook such as *The Certificate in Education and Training* (2014) by Ann Gravells and Susan Simpson. Reading that book may prove valuable in helping you increase your knowledge and understanding of teaching, training and assessment in the Further Education and Skills Sector.

This book will suit anyone taking the Certificate in Education and Training, whether as a short intensive programme of study, by attending a formal programme over a number of days or weeks, or by using a distance, open, online or blended learning approach. There are many optional units which can be taken as part of the Certificate; however, only the mandatory units are covered in detail in this book.

Chapters 1–19 contain self-assessment activities for you to carry out, together with guidance to help you demonstrate and evidence your achievement towards each learning outcome of the Certificate units. This book is not intended to give you the answers to questions you may be asked in any formal assessments; your responses will be *specific to you*, the *subject* you will teach and the *context* and *environment* in which you will teach. The Certificate's units are made up of *learning outcomes* and *assessment criteria* which are stated in each chapter. Learning outcomes are what you *will learn to do*, i.e. obtaining the required skills, knowledge and understanding, and assessment criteria are what you *can do*, i.e. putting it all into practice.

At the end of Chapters 1–19 is a completed assessment grid. Each grid gives examples of evidence you could provide to meet the assessment criteria. Evidence can be cross-referenced between the assessment criteria as there is some duplication between the units. The Certificate consists of five mandatory units, which can be achieved independently of each other or at the same time. Whilst the assessment grids will give guidance regarding evidencing each separate assessment criteria, you might be assessed more holistically, i.e. towards several of the assessment criteria at the same time. You will need to find out how you will be assessed at the organisation you are taking the qualification with.

Chapter 20 contains useful information regarding preparing for and carrying out your teaching practice, as well as being observed with your own learners.

For the purpose of this book, the generic term *teacher* is used, even though you might be called something different: for example, assessor, coach, counsellor, facilitator, instructor, lecturer, mentor, presenter, staff development manager, supervisor, trainer or tutor. The generic term *learner* is also used and refers to other terms such as apprentice, candidate, delegate, participant, pupil, student and trainee.

Appendix 1 shows the structure of the units which make up the Certificate in Education and Training.

The index at the back of the book will help you to locate relevant topics quickly.

Some of the regulations and organisations referred to in this book may only be relevant in England; therefore you will need to find out what is applicable to you if you work elsewhere.

Self-assessment activities and guidance for evidencing achievement

As you progress through your programme of study, you can work through the self-assessment activities in Chapters 1–19. Once you have completed the activities in the first part of each chapter, check your responses with the guidance in the second part of the chapter.

Each chapter relates to one of the 19 learning outcomes contained in the five units of the Certificate. Responding to these activities will help you focus upon the assessment criteria and guide you towards meeting the requirements of the units. The activities will address each individual assessment criterion of the units; however, you might be able to achieve several at the same time depending upon how you will be assessed.

As you work through the self-assessment activities, make sure your responses are *specific to you* and the *subject* you will teach. You should state the *context* and *environment* in which you will teach. Examples of the context could be:

- adult education
- armed, emergency and uniformed services
- charitable organisations
- community education
- further education colleges
- higher education institutions and universities
- immigration and detention centres
- on-site learning centres

- prisoner and offender centres
- private sector learning
- probation services
- public sector learning
- schools and academies
- sixth-form colleges
- voluntary sector learning
- work-based learning

Examples of the environment include classrooms, community halls, outdoor spaces, training rooms, workshops, the workplace, and anywhere else that teaching, learning and assessment can occur.

When responding to the questions, you could explain the documentation you use at work along with the relevant policies, procedures and guidelines you follow. You could produce a short case study of how you have demonstrated applying theory into practice – just make sure you anonymise it by not using any names of the organisations or your learners. You could also make a video of you and your learners to show how you have met various aspects of the qualification. You will need to obtain the permission of your organisation and your learners prior to doing so.

The Certificate in Education and Training

The Certificate in Education and Training is a teaching qualification achievable at level 4 on the Qualifications and Credit Framework (QCF). You will find more information on the QCF in the next section of this chapter.

The qualification is made up of different units to the value of 36 credits. Think of one credit as approximately 10 hours of learning; therefore 36 credits equates to 360 hours of learning. This will consist of a certain amount of *contact time* with your teacher such as attending sessions and being assessed. It also consists of your own time, known as *non-contact time* which can be used for reading, research, completing assignments and gathering evidence towards meeting the requirements of the qualification.

The qualification is made up of the following five mandatory units (which total 21 credits), plus optional units to the value of 15 credits. The first unit is at level 3 and is also part of the Award in Education and Training. If you have taken the Award prior to working towards the Certificate, you will not need to repeat this unit:

- Understanding roles, responsibilities and relationships in education and training (level 3)
- Planning to meet the needs of learners in education and training (level 4)
- Delivering education and training (level 4)
- Assessing learners in education and training (level 4)
- Using resources for education and training (level 4)

You are responsible for keeping up to date with the subject that you wish to teach. Whilst the book will help you with ideas for teaching and assessing in general, you will need to adapt these to suit your subject and the environment within which you will teach. Throughout your career, you might be known as a *dual professional*, i.e. a professional in the *subject* you will teach, as well as a professional *teacher*.

How you are assessed towards achievement of the Certificate will differ depending upon whom you are registered with. The organisation you are taking the qualification with will register you with an awarding organisation (AO). Each AO will specify how you will be assessed, for example, assignments, case studies, written work and projects. Some might have a more academic focus, i.e. require formal writing and the use of research and referencing. You will need to find out how you will be assessed before you commence, to ensure you can meet the requirements. Whilst the delivery and assessment methods might differ, the content of the qualification units will be the same no matter whom you are registered with.

Qualifications and Credit Framework

The Qualifications and Credit Framework (QCF) is a system for recognising skills and qualifications by awarding credit values to units of qualifications in England and Northern Ireland. The equivalent for Scotland is the Scottish Credit and Qualifications Framework (SCQF), and for Wales the Credit and Qualifications Framework for Wales (CQFW).

These credit values enable you to see how long it would take an average learner to achieve a unit. For example, the Understanding roles, responsibilities and relationships in education and training unit of the Certificate is 3 credits which equates to 30 hours. These hours include contact time with a teacher and assessor, and non-contact time for individual study and assignment work.

There are three sizes of qualifications in the QCF, each with a title and associated credit values:

- Award (1 to 12 credits)

- Certificate (13 to 36 credits)

- Diploma (37 credits or more)

All qualifications in the QCF use one of the above words in their title, for example, the Level 2 Award in Door Supervision, the Level 4 Certificate in Education and Training, and the Level 5 Diploma in Management. The level of the qualification defines how *difficult* it is to achieve and the credit value defines how long it will take to achieve.

You don't have to start with an Award, progress to a Certificate and then to a Diploma as all subjects are different. The terms award, certificate and Diploma relate to how *big* the qualification is (i.e. its size), which is based on the total number of credits. For example, a Diploma with 37 credits would equate to 370 hours of learning and is therefore a bigger qualification than an award with 12 credits and 120 hours of learning. The bigger the qualification, the longer it will take to achieve.

The QCF in England and Northern Ireland has 9 levels, ranging from entry level through levels 1 to 8 – for example, level 3 would be easier to achieve than level 6.

A rough comparison of the levels to other qualifications is:

1. GCSEs (grades D–G)

2. GCSEs (grades A*–C), Intermediate Apprenticeship

3. Advanced level (A level), Advanced Apprenticeship

4. Vocational Qualification level 4, Higher Apprenticeship

5. Vocational Qualification level 5, Foundation Degree

6. Bachelor's Degree

7. Master's Degree, Postgraduate Certificate and Diploma

8. Doctor of Philosophy (DPhil or PhD)

The chapters in this book will help you identify how you can demonstrate your achievements to meet the assessment criteria of the five main units of the Certificate.

Working towards the Certificate

To start the process of achieving your Certificate, you will need to enrol at a training organisation, college or other establishment that offers it. If you are currently teaching, your employer might inform you where you can take it and might also fund it for you. If you are not yet teaching (pre-service), you will need to find out where the Certificate is offered and apply for a place. You will need at least 30 hours of teaching practice – this could be part of your current teaching role if you are *in-service*, or perhaps voluntary work if you are *pre-service*. A quick search via the internet or a phone call to your local training organisation or college will soon locate providers which offer the Certificate. You might be interviewed and/or have to complete an application form. At this stage it would be useful to ask any questions or discuss any concerns you might have prior to commencing. You should also undertake an initial assessment, which might involve completing a form or having a discussion with your teacher. This will ascertain if you have any particular learning needs, for example, with English or maths, if you need help with study skills, or if you have any relevant prior skills and knowledge. You should always be honest so that you can be appropriately supported throughout your learning experience.

Depending upon where you have enrolled, the provider will explain how the programme will be delivered and assessed. It might be by attending formal sessions on a weekly or daily basis at a certain venue, or a mix of attending sessions combined with self-study materials. Other approaches might involve visiting you in your workplace, supporting you on a one-to-one basis, or a blended learning approach, for example, completing activities online via the internet, or working at home with occasional attendance at group sessions.

You will be allocated a designated teacher (who might also assess your work and observe your teaching practice) who will give you ongoing support, guidance and feedback throughout your time taking the Certificate. If you don't pass any assessments first time, you should be given the opportunity to discuss them with your assessor and have another attempt. The activities in this book will help you understand the content of the units of the Certificate and prepare you for the assessments. Please remember they are not a substitute for any formal assessments you will be given.

If you are an in-service teacher, it is good practice to be assigned a *mentor*. This is someone, preferably in the same organisation and subject area as yourself, who will be able to give you ongoing help, support and advice. Your organisation might allocate someone to you, but you may not feel comfortable with this, for example, if it's your line manager. Ideally, you should choose a person who can be objective with their help and advice, yet give you support in your subject area.

As you work through the units' requirements you should be informed regularly of your progress and you should have the opportunity to discuss any issues or concerns you may have. The work you produce towards achieving the assessment criteria of the units will be formally assessed and you will receive feedback regarding your progress and achievement. This feedback should confirm your achievements, or outline any further work you will be required to undertake.

A sample of your work might be *internally* and/or *externally quality assured*. Internal quality assurance (IQA) means that someone else who works in the same organisation where you are taking the Certificate will sample aspects of the assessment process. This is to ensure you have been assessed fairly and that your work has met the qualification requirements. External quality assurance (EQA) means that someone from the awarding organisation who issues your Certificate might also sample the assessment and internal quality assurance process.

Assessment criteria

All qualifications in the QCF contain assessment criteria. The assessment criteria of each of the Certificate's units begin with verbs; these are words which describe what you need to do to achieve them, for example, explain, summarise and use. When you are working towards them, you need to ensure you can meet the requirements.

Table 0.1 lists the verbs used in the Certificate units, with the action required to meet them. The self-assessment activities in this book are based on these verbs.

Table 0.1 Verbs used in the Certificate in Education and Training units

Verb	Action required
Adapt	Amend, change or revise something, for example, updating resources to meet the needs of learners
Analyse	Give a detailed structured and logical explanation or criticism of a subject, for example, why certain teaching and learning approaches did or did not work
Apply	Demonstrate theory in practice, for example, aspects of the minimum core such as literacy and language
Communicate	Actively engage and involve others, for example, to meet the individual needs of learners
Conduct	Implement something, for example, to assess learners
Create	Develop something, for example, an inclusive learning environment
Demonstrate	Use examples to put theory into practice, for example, to show how you create an inclusive learning environment
Describe	Give a detailed account of something, for example, the different agencies or people to whom you could refer learners
Design	Produce something, for example, a teaching and learning plan for a session
Devise	Create and develop something, for example, a scheme of work
Explain	Describe the facts of something and give detailed examples, for example, the roles and responsibilities of a teacher
Identify	Give the defining characteristics of something, for example, the different ways that constructive feedback can be given

Verb	Action required
Record	Document something, for example, learners' progress and achievements
Review	Critically appraise something, for example, a well-considered evaluation of how effective your practice is, with examples of what went well, what didn't and why
Summarise	Give a short account of the main facts of the topics in question, for example, the key aspects of legislation relevant to your specialist subject
Use	Demonstrate the use of something, for example, technology during sessions

Assessment methods and activities

Each awarding organisation will design its own assessment strategy for the Certificate; therefore the methods and activities used to assess you might vary depending upon whom you are registered with. You will need to meet all the learning outcomes and assessment criteria for the units you are taking. This will be by demonstrating your skills, knowledge and understanding, and putting theory into practice with your learners.

Your assessor will give you feedback regarding your progress and achievement. You might be able to submit a draft of your work first, for informal feedback, before submitting your final work for assessment. If you don't pass, you should be referred, usually with the opportunity to resubmit your work within a set timescale.

Some of the assessment methods used for the Certificate are:

- Assessment grids
- Assignments
- Case studies
- Checklists
- Essays
- Observations
- Online assessments
- Portfolio of evidence
- Professional discussion
- Projects
- Questions – written, oral, online
- Reflective learning journal
- Self-evaluation and action plan
- Written tasks/written statements
- Worksheets

You might be assessed by one or more of the methods through several different activities. Alternatively you might be assessed *holistically*, i.e. having the opportunity to demonstrate several assessment criteria from different units at the same time. If you are in any doubt as to how you will be assessed, or the target dates for the submission of your work, you will need to talk to your teacher or assessor.

The assessment methods are briefly explained here. However, you will need to clarify with your teacher or assessor any specific requirements which will relate to you.

Assessment grids

An assessment grid contains all the Certificate's learning outcomes and assessment criteria for each of the units. You will need to write how you have met the criteria and/or link them to documents and evidence from your teaching practice.

It might be possible to meet the requirements of several assessment criteria from different units at the same time. If this is the case, you will be able to cross-reference your work rather than repeat it. For example, the resources you use might demonstrate aspects from other units and assessment criteria. An example of a completed assessment grid can be seen after each chapter in this book.

Assignments

An assignment should ensure that all the assessment criteria can be met through various tasks or problem-solving activities. These might not be in the same order as the Certificate's assessment criteria; however, you should be able to complete all the requirements as you progress through your programme of study. The assignment will assess your knowledge and how you can apply it, perhaps through answering questions, group discussions, presentations to peers, and evidence of your teaching practice. You will need time for self-reflection to consolidate your learning as you progress through the assignment. You will be given a target date for completion, and possibly a word count for all written work. Your assessor should give you ongoing feedback and if you don't fully meet the criteria, you should be given the opportunity to have another attempt.

Case studies

A case study usually consists of a hypothetical or imaginary event for you to analyse. You can then make suggestions regarding how you would deal with the event, which should relate to the assessment criteria.

Alternatively, you could produce your own case study regarding a real situation that you have encountered, again relating it to the assessment criteria, but keeping it anonymous by not using any names of organisations or your learners.

Checklists

A checklist is a list of aspects which need to be achieved which will relate to the assessment criteria. They can be used by you as a form of self-assessment to check your progress so far, or by your assessor to confirm your achievement at a given point. They can be completed and dated when the relevant assessment criteria have been met. Checklists are often used in conjunction with other assessment methods.

Essays

Essays are formal pieces of writing to meet the requirements of the Certificate. There will usually be a word count to ensure you remain focused and specific, and you might be able to go 10% above or below the figure given. You will have a target date for submission and if you can't meet this for any reason, make sure you discuss this with your assessor.

You will usually have to word process your work in a professional style; however, if it is acceptable for you to handwrite your responses, make sure your writing is legible and neatly written. Your assessor should give you guidance as to how to present your work. Always check your spelling, grammar, punctuation and sentence structure. Try not to rely on your computer to check these as it doesn't always realise the context within which you are writing.

Essays often include quoting from relevant textbooks, websites and journals. How to do this is explained briefly towards the end of this chapter.

Observations

At some point, you will be observed delivering sessions with your learners, usually for an hour on three separate occasions. However, some optional units have additional observation requirements, for example, the unit Assess occupational competence in the work environment. As this unit is also part of the Learning and Development suite of qualifications, further assessment requirements apply. After the observation you should receive feedback from your assessor. This feedback should also be given to you in written form, either electronic or a hard copy. You need to consider the feedback you have received when evaluating your delivery.

Teaching practice is a chance to use your newfound skills and knowledge with your learners. Never be afraid to try something new or do something differently if it didn't work the first time. No teaching situation is ever the same, as you will have different learners on different occasions. What works for one learner or group, might not work with another.

Throughout the level 4 units of the Certificate, you are required to demonstrate the *Minimum Core elements*. These are your personal skills in literacy, language, numeracy and information and communication technology (ICT).

Some examples of integrating elements of these skills into your sessions are:

- *literacy* – reading, writing, spelling, grammar, punctuation, syntax

- *language* – speaking, listening, discussing, role play, interviews

- *numeracy* – calculations, interpretations, evaluations, measurements

- *ICT* – online applications, e-learning programs, word processing, use of an interactive whiteboard and/or virtual learning environment (VLE), writing emails, using video conferencing, podcasts and other aspects of new technology

Your observer will be looking for examples of how you demonstrate these.

Whilst you are taking the Certificate you may find it useful to arrange to observe your mentor if you have one, or another teacher or assessor in the same subject area as yourself. This will help you to see how they plan, prepare, deliver, assess and evaluate their session, which should give you some useful ideas.

Online assessments

An online assessment is where you submit your work via the internet to an assessor. You will either email your work or upload it to a learning portal via a dedicated website. There are many online learning sites available. One of the most popular is known as a virtual learning environment (VLE) which is based on Moodle. Moodle stands for a Modular Object-Oriented Dynamic Learning Environment. These sites also enable you to communicate with your assessor and your peers and to view resources and supporting learning materials.

If you are taking the Certificate totally via an online programme, you might not meet the assessor who will give you feedback concerning your work. You will therefore need to stay in touch regularly and communicate any issues or concerns to them. This might be by email, telephone or other means. You will still have to be observed, but this might be by someone other than your online assessor. You will need to communicate regularly with your assessor and observer, for example, if you can't meet a target date, or you need to change an observation date.

Online assessment can include *formative* (ongoing) assessment, i.e. obtaining feedback from your assessor regarding a draft submission of your work. This feedback will help confirm if you are making good progress or advise you of any areas you need to improve. You could then upload your completed work for *summative* (final) assessment when you have completed it.

Please see the assignments and essays paragraphs for information regarding how to produce your work.

Portfolio of evidence

A portfolio of evidence contains proof of your achievement towards meeting the assessment criteria. This could be electronic (for example, computer folders containing various files and documents), or manual (for example, hard copies of documents placed in a ring binder or folder). These will include statements as to how you have met the assessment criteria, along with documents such as your scheme of work, observation reports and resources. When producing a portfolio, consider quality not quantity. If you have re-submitted any work, you will need to include your original work as well as your revised work.

Professional discussion

A professional discussion is a conversation with your assessor in which you justify how you have achieved the assessment criteria. Your assessor might verbally explore your knowledge and understanding of the teaching role rather than your having to write about it. Having a professional discussion with your assessor is a good way to demonstrate how you have met the assessment criteria if you are having difficulty expressing yourself through written work.

A professional discussion can be used as an *holistic* assessment method, meaning several criteria can be assessed at the same time. Your assessor will prompt you to explain how you have met the requirements and ask to see documents which confirm this. They might make written notes during the discussion and/or make a visual or aural recording (often digitally) of your conversation, if appropriate, which can be kept as evidence of your achievement. Prior to the professional discussion taking place, you should agree with your assessor the nature of the content of the conversation to enable you to prepare in advance. You may need to bring along examples of teaching materials you have prepared and used. When you are having the professional discussion try and remain focused, don't digress but be specific with your responses. At the end of the discussion, your assessor should confirm which assessment criteria you have achieved, and which you still need to work towards.

Projects

A project usually consists of practical activities which can be carried out during your teaching practice and will be based on the assessment criteria. You should be given a target date for completion, and possibly a word count for any written work. Projects usually take longer in terms of time than an assignment, and might group several assessment criteria together.

Questions – written, oral, online

You may need to produce answers to written or oral questions which will be based around the assessment criteria of the units. You might need to complete these using a word processor, by keying in responses online, or by recording them digitally.

Please see the assignments and essays paragraphs for information on how to produce written work.

If you have answered a written question and met most but not all of the assessment criteria, your assessor might ask you some oral questions to ensure you have the relevant knowledge and understanding to fill any gaps.

Reflective learning journal

A reflective learning journal is a way of helping you formally focus upon your learning, progress and achievement towards the Certificate. You might be given a template or a document to complete, or you could write in a diary, use a journal or a notebook, or use a word processor. When you write, make sure your work is legible as your assessor will need to read and understand it. Try and reflect upon your experiences by analysing as well as describing them and be as specific as possible as to how your experiences have met the assessment criteria. You can reflect upon your experiences as a learner taking the Certificate, and as a teacher regarding your experiences with your learners. You could annotate your writing with the assessment criteria numbers such as 1.1, 1.2, 1.3, etc. to show which criteria you feel you have achieved from the relevant units. Don't just write a chronological account of events; consider what worked well, or didn't work well, and how you could do something differently given the opportunity. You will need to make sure you address the verbs of each of the assessment criteria, see pages 6 and 7 for examples.

Reflection should become a part of your everyday activities and enable you to look at things in detail that you perhaps would not ordinarily do. There may be events you would not want to change or improve if you felt they went well. If this is the case, reflect as to why they went well and use similar situations in future sessions. As you become more experienced at reflective writing, you will see how you can make improvements to benefit your learners and yourself.

Self-evaluation and action plan

A self-evaluation and action plan is normally based on a template or document which you will complete at the end of each unit and/or at the end of taking the Certificate. Your writing should clearly evaluate your progress and achievement regarding how you have met the learning outcomes and assessment criteria. The action plan will help you focus upon the skills, knowledge and understanding required for your personal development in the future. This could be by considering what other programmes you could take, for example, to improve your computer skills, and what other books, journals or websites you might access to help with your continuing professional development (CPD).

Written tasks/written statements

Written tasks or written statements are a way of demonstrating how you have met the required assessment criteria by giving specific examples of what you have done. You might address individual questions which directly relate to each of the assessment criteria, or answer one question which addresses several assessment criteria holistically.

Please see the assignments and essays paragraphs for information on how to produce your work.

Worksheets

Worksheets are like handouts and include tasks, activities and/or questions for you to carry out. These can be completed during attended sessions, in your own time or online. Worksheets are often used to check progress and might link several assessment criteria together. After completing them, your assessor will check whether your responses can be used to demonstrate achievement of the relevant assessment criteria, and give you constructive feedback to help you develop further.

Referencing work

As the Certificate is at level 4, you will be required to use quotes from relevant sources such as textbooks, journals and websites when submitting your written work for assessment. This is known as *referencing* and shows that you have read relevant information and related it to your efforts. If you are required to do this, you will need to check with your assessor which writing style to use, and whether it is mandatory or optional to use it. The *Harvard* system is the style that is generally used and standardises the approach to writing and referencing. However, other styles could be used within your writing; just make sure you are consistent throughout your work regarding layout and punctuation.

It is important to reference your work to:

- acknowledge the work of other writers, authors and theorists

- assist the reader to locate your sources for their own reference, and to confirm they are correct

- avoid plagiarism (i.e. using the work of others without acknowledging it)

- provide evidence of your reading and research

- use existing knowledge and theories to support your writing (whether as a direct quote or paraphrased into your own words)

Referencing a book

When using quotes from different sources, for example, a textbook, you need to insert *the author, date of publication* and *page number* after any quotation you have used. The full details of the book can then be included in a *reference list* at the end of your work.

For example, if you are describing ground rules, you could state:

> Ground rules should be agreed at the start of a new programme. 'Ground rules can be used to create suitable conditions within which learners can safely work and learn' (Gravells, 2013: 100). It is important to establish these early to ensure the programme runs smoothly. If learners do not feel safe, they might not return again, or their learning could be affected.

Any quote you insert within your text should be within quotation marks, often known as speech marks. The name of the author, the year of publication of the book and the page number should be in brackets directly afterwards. At the end of your work, you should have a reference list in alphabetical order, giving the full details of the book from which you have quoted. For example:

Reference list

Gravells, A (2013) The Award in Education and Training. London: Learning Matters SAGE.

When inserting a quote, make sure you understand what the quote means and how it will fit within your writing. It could be that you agree with what the author has said and it supports what you are saying, or it could be that you totally disagree with it. If so, explain why you agree or disagree and, if it's the latter, state what you would do differently. You need to write what you think, or what your point of view is, and relate it to your specialist subject.

Throughout your writing, you should refer to different sources and authors where applicable. The organisation you are taking the Certificate with should be able to give you advice regarding using quotes and referencing your work, and provide you with a reading list of relevant textbooks.

It is advisable to use a range of sources to develop your knowledge and understanding. Reading more than one book will help you to gain the perspectives of different authors. You don't have to read the book fully, you can just locate relevant topics by using the index at the back of the book. If you have a look at the index at the back of this book, you will see all the topics are listed alphabetically, making it easy for you to locate the relevant page numbers.

If the quote is longer than three lines of text, indent the paragraph from both margins. Three dots ... can be used to indicate words you have left out. Always copy the words and punctuation as it is in the original, even if there are spelling mistakes. You can add [*sic*] after the error to denote you are aware of it. Long quotes are always in single line spacing, quotes of three lines or less can be in the line spacing of the main text, for example, if you have used double line spacing.

If a quote is not used, but the author is still referred to, it will look like this:

> *Gravells (2013) advocates the use of ground rules with learners.*

Again, the full book details will go in the reference list.

Referencing a website

The quote would be inserted within your writing in a similar way to a textbook quote.

For example:

> *'There is no one single strategy for creating assessments suitable for learners who have difficulty communicating with others, due to the wide range of conditions and impairments that might lead to such a difficulty' (LSIS, 2012).*

It would look like this in your reference list, along with the date it was accessed:

> *Learning and Skills Information Service (2012) http://www.excellencegateway.org.uk/node/320 (accessed 16.05.13)*

The date you accessed it is important, as web pages often change or are removed.

Referencing an online report

The quote would be inserted within your writing in the same way as a textbook quote.

For example:

> *'Teacher educators have traditionally struggled with convincing learners to work on their portfolios, competing against more traditional assessment demands and the habit of putting the portfolio together at the last minute' (Hopper and Sanford, 2010: 4).*

It would look like this in your reference list, along with the date it was accessed:

> *Hopper, T and Sanford, K (2010) 'Starting a program-wide e-portfolio practice in teacher education: resistance, support and renewal', Teacher Education Quarterly, special online edition http://www.teq-journal.org/onlineissue/PDFFlash/HopperSanfordManuscript/fscommand/Hopper_Sanford.pdf (accessed 16.05.13)*

There are other ways of referencing different sources of information and you might like to obtain further information from relevant textbooks or websites to help you.

Study skills and reflective practice

When studying for your Certificate, you will need to be prepared to use your own time for activities such as research, reading textbooks, completing assessments and assignments, and reflecting upon your practice. You will need to be self-motivated and able to dedicate an appropriate amount of time to this. If you can, set aside time in a place where you won't be disturbed so that you can focus on what is required. If you are interrupted, distracted, hungry or thirsty when studying, you probably won't be able to concentrate very well. You will need to keep to any target dates for submitting your assessments, and inform your assessor if you can't meet any. Using a diary to forward plan when these need submitting will help when planning your time. You could also use your diary to note down details of critical events to enable you to reflect on them later.

Study skills

To help you study effectively, it's useful to know the best ways in which to learn. You will probably have a particular learning preference, a way that suits you best. For example, you might like to watch someone perform a task, and then carry it out for yourself, or you might just want to try it out for yourself first. Most people can be grouped into four styles of learning: visual, aural, read/write and kinaesthetic, known by the acronym VARK. If you have access to the internet, go to www.vark-learn.com and carry out the short online questionnaire. See what your results are for each of V, A, R and K and read how you can learn more effectively.

If you are attending a taught programme, it would be useful to make notes during your sessions to which you can refer later. This could be on handouts given by your teacher, or hard copies of a presentation. If you have a laptop or tablet, you could make notes electronically during the session (providing this is acceptable). When making notes, try to remain focused, otherwise you might miss something. You could write quickly by cutting out vowels, for example, *tchr* for *teacher*. You could also cut out small words such as *an*, *are*, *at*, *is* and *the*. Whichever way you take notes, make sure you will know what they mean when you look back at them. If you are reading handouts, textbooks and/or journals, you might like to use a highlighter pen or underline certain words to draw attention to them. You could also make notes in the margins, but only do this on your own materials, not on ones borrowed from others or libraries. If you are using the latter, you could use sticky notes instead.

During attended programmes, you might be required to take part in group work or give short presentations to your peers. Use this as an opportunity to work with others and to gain new skills and knowledge. If you are taking the Certificate via an online or distance learning programme, you might not meet your teacher or your peers in person. However, you should be able to communicate with them either by email or through an internet-based system.

You might need support to help you improve aspects such as English, maths and computer skills. This might be available at the organisation where you are taking the Certificate, or you could attend other relevant programmes. There are some free online programmes available that you could access and which are listed at the end of this chapter. If you don't have access to a computer at home, you could use one at a local library or an internet cafe. Most smart phones enable you to download applications which might be appropriate.

If you are unsure of anything whilst you are studying, or have any concerns, don't be afraid to ask for help. It's best that you get clarification prior to submitting any work for assessment, in case you have misinterpreted something.

Although this is a very brief guide to study skills, you might like to obtain further information from relevant textbooks or websites to help you. If you are ever in any doubt, talk to your assessor and ask for advice.

Reflective practice

Reflection is a way of reviewing your own progress, which is often just your thoughts (which can be positive or negative) but can take into account feedback you have received from others. It is useful to maintain a reflective learning journal or a diary to note critical events; you can then refer to these when planning your future development and preparing your sessions. Reflecting upon the effectiveness of your practice is part of the four mandatory units of the Certificate which are at level 4. You will therefore need to keep evidence of your reflections throughout your time taking the programme.

Reflection is about becoming more self-aware, which should give you increased confidence and improve the links between the theory and practice of teaching, learning and assessment.

A straightforward method of reflection is to have the *experience*, then *describe it, analyse* it and *revise* it (EDAR). This method incorporates the *who, what, when, where, why* and *how* approach (WWWWWWH) and should help you consider ways of changing and/or improving:

Experience → Describe → Analyse → Revise

EDAR

- *Experience* – a significant event or incident you would like to change or improve.

- *Describe* – aspects such as *who* was involved, *what* happened, *when* it happened and *where* it happened.

- *Analyse* – consider the experience more deeply and ask yourself *how* it happened and *why* it happened.

- *Revise* – think about how you would do it differently if it happened again and then try this out if you have the opportunity (Gravells, 2013a: 186).

Self-reflection should become a part of your everyday activities, enabling you to analyse and focus on things in greater detail. All reflection should lead to an improvement in your practice; however, there may be events you would not want to change or improve as you felt they went well. If this is the case, reflect as to why they went well and use these methods in future sessions. If you are not able to write a reflective learning journal, mentally run through the EDAR points in your head when you have time. As you become more experienced at reflective practice, you will see how you can improve and develop further.

Schön (1983) suggests two methods:

- reflection *in* action

- reflection *on* action

Reflection in action happens at the time of the incident, is often unconscious, is proactive and allows immediate changes to take place.

Reflection on action takes place after the incident, is a more conscious process and is reactive. This allows you time to think about the incident, consider a different approach, or to talk to others about it before making any changes. However, it might not allow you to deal with a situation as it occurs.

There are various theories regarding reflection which will be referred to throughout the chapters within this book.

The process of self-reflection and your own further development should help improve the quality of the service you give your learners.

Summary

In this chapter you have learnt about:

- the structure of the book and how to use it

- self-assessment activities and guidance for evidencing achievement

- the Certificate in Education and Training

- assessment methods and activities

- referencing work

- study skills and reflective practice

Theory focus

References and further information

Directorate of Learning Resources (2010) *Harvard Referencing: Student Style Guide.* Sunderland: COSC Press.

Gravells, A (2012) *What is Teaching in the Lifelong Learning Sector?* London: Learning Matters SAGE.

Gravells, A (2013a) *The Award in Education and Training.* London: Learning Matters SAGE.

Gravells, A (2013b) *Passing the Award in Education and Training.* London: Learning Matters SAGE.

Gravells, A and Simpson, S (2014) *The Certificate in Education and Training.* London: Learning Matters SAGE.

Hargreaves, S (2012) *Study Skills for Students with Dyslexia.* London: SAGE Publications.

Malthouse, R and Roffey-Barentsen, J (2013) *Academic Skills: Contemporary Education Studies.* London: Thalassa Publishing.

Pears, R and Shields, G (2010) *Cite Them Right: The Essential Referencing Guide.* Basingstoke: Palgrave Macmillan.

Roffey-Barentsen, J and Malthouse, R (2013) *Reflective Practice in Education and Training* (2nd edn). London: Learning Matters SAGE.

Rushton, I and Suter, M (2012) *Reflective Practice for Teaching in Lifelong Learning.* Maidenhead: OU Press.

Schön, D (1983) *The Reflective Practitioner: How Professionals Think in Action.* New York: Basic Books.

Websites

Ann Gravells (information and resources) – www.anngravells.co.uk

Awarding organisations – www.ofqual.gov.uk/for-awarding-organisations

Computer free support – www.onlinebasics.co.uk and http://learn.go-on.co.uk

Credit and Qualification Framework for Wales (CQFW) – www.cqfw.org

Digital Unite – http://digitalunite.com/guides

English and maths free support – www.move-on.org.uk

Learning preference questionnaire – www.vark-learn.com

Minimum Core Standards – http://repository.excellencegateway.org.uk/fedora/objects/import-pdf:93/datastreams/PDF/content

Minimum Core – inclusive learning approaches for literacy, language, numeracy and ICT (2007) – http://www.excellencegateway.org.uk/node/12020

Qualifications and Credit Framework (QCF) shortcut – http://tinyurl.com/447bgy2

Online free courses in various subjects – www.vision2learn.net

Post Compulsory Education and Training Network – www.pcet.net

Scottish Credit and Qualifications Framework (SCQF) – www.scqf.org.uk

Teacher training videos – www.teachertrainingvideos.com

Videos by Ann Gravells – http://www.youtube.com/channel/UCEQQRbP7x4L7NAy4wsQi7jA

1 UNDERSTAND THE TEACHING ROLE AND RESPONSIBILITIES IN EDUCATION AND TRAINING

This chapter is in two parts. The first part: **Self-assessment activities**, contains questions and activities which relate to the first learning outcome of the Certificate in Education and Training unit Understanding roles, responsibilities and relationships in education and training.

The assessment criteria are shown in boxes and are followed by questions and activities for you to carry out. Ensure your responses are *specific to you*, the *subject* you will teach and the *context* and *environment* in which you will teach. This unit is at level 3 and therefore does not require academic writing and referencing skills to be demonstrated. The other mandatory units are at level 4.

After completing the activities, check your responses with the second part: **Guidance for evidencing achievement**. This guidance is not intended to give you the answers to questions you may be asked in any formal assessments; however, it will help you focus your responses towards meeting the assessment criteria.

At the end of the chapter is an example of a completed **Assessment grid** which gives ideas for evidence you could provide towards meeting the assessment criteria. Evidence can be cross-referenced between units and assessment criteria if it meets the requirements.

Self-assessment activities

> 1.1 Explain the teaching role and responsibilities in education and training

Q1 Explain what you consider your role as a teacher will be, and the responsibilities you will have.

> 1.2 Summarise key aspects of legislation, regulatory requirements and codes of practice relating to own role and responsibilities

Q2 What legislation, regulatory requirements and codes of practice must you follow to teach your subject?

Q3 Summarise the key aspects of those you have mentioned in your response to Q2.

1.3 Explain ways to promote equality and value diversity

Q4 What do the terms equality and diversity mean?

Q5 Explain how you could promote equality and value diversity with your learners.

1.4 Explain why it is important to identify and meet individual learner needs

Q6 Why is it important to identify the needs of learners and how can you do this?

Q7 List at least four examples of learner needs and explain how you could meet them.

Guidance for evidencing achievement

1.1 Explain the teaching role and responsibilities in education and training

Q1 Explain what you consider your role as a teacher will be, and the responsibilities you will have.

Your response could explain that your main role should be to teach or train your subject in a way which actively involves and engages your learners during every session, whether this is in the workplace, in a college or other training environment. However, it's not just about teaching and training, it's about the learning that takes place as a result. You can teach as much as you wish, but if learning is not taking place then your teaching has not been successful. Therefore you must also carry out some form of assessment to find this out.

Part of your role should be to help your learners achieve their chosen programme or qualification. This will be by using various teaching, learning and assessment approaches, and taking individual learner needs into account.

You could go on to explain your other roles and responsibilities, some of which are listed alphabetically here:

- attending meetings

- carrying out relevant administrative requirements

- communicating appropriately and effectively with learners and others

- completing attendance records/registers

- complying with relevant regulatory requirements, legislation, policies and procedures, and codes of practice

- differentiating teaching, learning and assessment approaches and materials

- ensuring assessment decisions are valid, reliable, fair and ethical

- ensuring learners are on the right programme at the right level

- establishing ground rules by negotiation

- following health and safety, equality and diversity, and safeguarding requirements

- giving appropriate information, advice and guidance where necessary

- helping learners develop their English, maths, and information and communication technology (ICT) skills

- incorporating new technology where possible

- maintaining a safe, positive and accessible learning environment for learners and others

- maintaining records and confidentiality where applicable

- partaking in quality assurance processes

- participating proactively in any external audits or inspections

- promoting appropriate behaviour and respect for others

- recording and monitoring learners' progress against their targets and learning goals

- referring learners to other people or agencies when necessary

- reflecting on your own practice and partaking in professional development activities

- standardising your practice with others

- teaching, training and assessing in an inclusive, engaging and motivating way

- using a variety of assessment types and methods to assess progress formally and informally, and giving feedback to learners

- using appropriate equipment and resources

- using icebreakers and energisers effectively

You could obtain your job description and use a highlight pen to identify your role and responsibilities.

1.2 Summarise key aspects of legislation, regulatory requirements and codes of practice relating to own role and responsibilities

---

Q2 What legislation, regulatory requirements and codes of practice must you follow to teach your subject?

These will differ depending upon the subject you wish to teach, and the context and environment within which you will teach. However, your response could include a generic list of legislation such as:

- Copyright Designs and Patents Act (1988)

- Data Protection Act (1998)

- Equality Act (2010)

- Health and Safety at Work etc. Act (1974)

- Safeguarding Vulnerable Groups Act (2006)

You should then state the regulatory requirements which relate to your specific subject such as:

- Control of Substances Hazardous to Health (COSHH) Regulations (2002) for subjects which include the use of chemicals and hazardous materials

- Food Hygiene Regulations (2006) for subjects which include the use of food

- Health and Safety (Display Screen Equipment) Regulations (1992) for subjects which include the use of a computer screen

- Manual Handling Operation Regulations (1992) for subjects which include the lifting and carrying of items

You should then state the Codes of Practice which relate to the organisation in which you will teach, as well as any associations or professional bodies you might belong to, such as:

- acceptable use of information technology

- code of conduct

- environmental awareness

- sustainability

- timekeeping

Q3 Summarise the key aspects of those you have mentioned in your response to Q2.

Your response should summarise the ones you have listed. For example, the Copyright Designs and Patents Act (1988) relates to the copying, adapting and distributing of materials, which includes computer programs and materials found via the internet. Organisations may have a licence to enable the photocopying of small amounts from books or journals. All copies should have the original source acknowledged.

The Control of Substances Hazardous to Health (COSHH) Regulations (2002) applies if you work with hazardous materials such as those used by hairdressing learners for colouring clients' hair. Employers are legally obliged to assess all potential hazards related to the work activity, and employees are required to prevent or adequately control the risks that are identified.

The Code of Practice regarding Acceptable use of Information Technology will be written in a format specific to your organisation. If you can access a copy, you could explain how it ensures that all staff and learners are aware of how information technology should be accessed and used, based on principles of honesty, integrity and respect for others. The Code of Practice should comply with relevant policies and legislation. However, organisations cannot always protect users from the presence of material they may find offensive.

1.3 Explain ways to promote equality and value diversity

Q4 What do the terms equality and diversity mean?

Your response could state that equality is about the rights of learners to have access to, attend, participate, make progress and succeed towards their chosen learning experience. This should be regardless of ability and/or circumstances.

Diversity is about valuing and respecting the differences in learners, regardless of ability and/or circumstances, or any other individual characteristics they may have.

You could relate your response to equality of opportunity, which is a concept underpinned by the Equality Act (2010) to provide relevant and appropriate access for the participation, development and advancement of all individuals and groups.

The Equality Act (2010) replaced all previous anti-discrimination legislation and consolidated it into one Act (for England, Scotland and Wales). It provides rights for people not to be directly discriminated against or harassed because they have an association with a disabled person or because they are wrongly perceived as disabled.

To ensure you comply with the Equality Act (2010), you need to be proactive in all aspects of equality and diversity. You should make sure your delivery style, teaching, learning and assessment resources promote and include all learners in respect of the Act's nine protected characteristics (known as personal attributes):

- age

- disability

- gender

- gender reassignment

- marriage and civil partnership

- race

- religion and belief

- sexual orientation

- pregnancy and maternity

Q5 Explain how you could promote equality and value diversity with your learners.

Your response should explain how you could promote equality and value diversity with your own learners, for example, promoting positive behaviour and respect by negotiating and agreeing ground rules with learners from the start of the programme. Another example is that you would challenge prejudice, discrimination and stereotyping as it occurs. You can also help your learners by organising the environment to enable ease of access around any obstacles (including other learners' bags and coats), and around internal and external doors. If you are ever in doubt as to how to help a learner, just ask them. Enhancing your learners' knowledge includes using appropriate resources, for example, pictures in handouts and presentations which reflect different abilities, ages, cultures, genders and races. Discussions can also take place to enhance knowledge which can often occur naturally rather than being planned. For example, if a learner mentions something which is relevant, and you feel it could be discussed further.

Incorporating activities based around equality and diversity, and the local community and society within which your learners live and work could help your learners be more understanding and tolerant of each other. Try and have discussions regarding your subject which are based on areas of your learners' interest, i.e. cultural topics, popular television programmes and relevant news stories. Place the responsibility on them to choose the topics rather than you. This should get them thinking about the concept of equality and diversity in society, and how to be accepting and tolerant of others. Using naturally occurring opportunities to explore aspects such as Ramadan or Chinese New Year when they occur will also help your learners appreciate and value diversity.

You could explain how you will ensure all learners have access to learning, not only physical access, but ensuring teaching, learning and assessment materials are suitable. For example, producing resources in different formats, i.e. hard copy and/or electronic.

> 1.4 Explain why it is important to identify and meet individual learner needs

Q6 Why is it important to identify the needs of learners and how can you do this?

Your response could explain that the importance of identifying learners' needs is to ensure they can be suitably met. Meeting their needs should help create an effective learning environment. Knowing what a learner's needs are will help you provide any necessary help and guidance. This should hopefully result in the learner being effectively supported throughout the learning programme. However, it may identify that the learner needs to work on certain skills, i.e. English, before applying for the programme. It is essential that the learner believes they can succeed from the start.

You should explain how you can identify the individual needs of your learners at your organisation. For example, by communicating with the learner prior to their commencing the programme, as part of the initial assessment process, during discussions at the interview stage, or during tutorial reviews.

For example, to identify if a learner has dyslexia, you could look for some of the indicators in adults which include:

- a low opinion of their capability
- difficulty filling in forms and writing reports
- difficulty structuring work schedules
- losing and forgetting things
- the tendency to miss and confuse appointment times

If you notice any of these, you could arrange for the learner to take a dyslexia test, the results of which will help you offer appropriate support to meet their needs. Your organisation might be able to arrange this or you could find out further information from the Dyslexia Association's website: www.dyslexia.uk.net.

Q7 List at least four examples of learner needs and explain how you could meet them.

Your list might include learners requiring support with:

- dyslexia, dyscalculia, dysgraphia or dyspraxia
- English as a second or other language
- family or personal concerns
- financial issues
- health concerns

Your response should then explain how you could meet the learners' needs you have listed, for example, what you would do to support a learner who has dyslexia. You could photocopy handouts on to different coloured paper, pastel often helps, or place handouts in a coloured plastic wallet for them. You could also offer to supply handouts and course materials in electronic format, enabling the learner to view, save and/or print them in a size, font and colour to suit their needs. Rather than singling out the particular learner, you could do the same for all learners.

If you are currently teaching, you could produce a case study of how you have met a particular learner's needs. However, make sure you don't use their names.

Theory focus

References and further information

Ayers, H and Gray, F (2006) *An A to Z Practical Guide to Learning Difficulties*. London: David Fulton Publishers.

Clark, T (2010) *Mental Health Matters for FE: Teachers Toolkit*. Leicester: NIACE.

Farrell, M (2006) *Dyslexia and Other Learning Difficulties*. London: Routledge.

Gravells, A and Simpson, S (2014) *The Certificate in Education and Training*. London: Learning Matters SAGE.

Gravells, A (2013) *The Award in Education and Training*. London: Learning Matters SAGE.

Gravells, A and Simpson, S (2012) *Equality and Diversity in the Lifelong Learning Sector* (2nd edn). London: Learning Matters SAGE.

Powell, S and Tummons, J (2011) *Inclusive Practice in the Lifelong Learning Sector*. London: Learning Matters SAGE.

Reece, I and Walker, S (2007) *Teaching, Training and Learning: A Practical Guide* (6th edn). Tyne & Wear: Business Education Publishers.

Wallace, S (2011) *Teaching, Tutoring and Training in the Lifelong Learning Sector* (4th edn). London: Learning Matters SAGE.

Websites

Dyslexia Association – www.dyslexia.uk.net

Equality Act (2010) – http://www.homeoffice.gov.uk/equalities/equality-act/

Equality and Diversity Forum – www.edf.org.uk

Government legislation – www.legislation.gov.uk

Initial and diagnostic assessment – http://archive.excellencegateway.org.uk/page.aspx?o=BSFAlearning difficulty%2Finitialassess

Regulatory requirements – http://standards.gov/regulations.cfm

UNIT TITLE: Understanding roles, responsibilities and relationships in education and training

Assessment grid

Learning Outcomes The learner will:	Assessment Criteria The learner can:		Example evidence
1. Understand the teaching role and responsibilities in education and training	1.1	Explain the teaching role and responsibilities in education and training	An explanation of the roles and responsibilities of a teacher in education and training, such as teaching and assessing, attending meetings, carrying out relevant administrative requirements, communicating appropriately, completing attendance records/registers.
			Your job description if you are currently in a teaching role, which highlights your role and responsibilities.
	1.2	Summarise key aspects of legislation, regulatory requirements and codes of practice relating to own role and responsibilities	A list of legislation, regulatory requirements and codes of practice relevant to your role and responsibilities as a teacher/trainer such as the Equality Act (2010), the Health and Safety at Work etc. Act (1974).
			A summary of the key aspects of those you have listed above.
	1.3	Explain ways to promote equality and value diversity	An explanation of what equality and diversity mean.
			An explanation of how you could promote equality and value diversity with your learners, with examples, such as discussing topics in the news.
			A summary of the Equality Act (2010) and how it could impact upon teaching, learning and assessment.
	1.4	Explain why it is important to identify and meet individual learner needs	An explanation of why it is important to identify your learners' needs such as to give appropriate support.
			An explanation of how to identify needs such as using initial assessments, interviews and discussions.
			A list of examples of learners' needs such as dyslexia, dyspraxia, English as a second or other language, family or personal concerns, financial issues, health concerns.
			An explanation of how you could meet the needs listed above.
			An anonymised case study of how you have met a particular learner's needs.

27

2 UNDERSTAND WAYS TO MAINTAIN A SAFE AND SUPPORTIVE LEARNING ENVIRONMENT

This chapter is in two parts. The first part: **Self-assessment activities**, contains questions and activities which relate to the second learning outcome of the Certificate in Education and Training unit Understanding roles, responsibilities and relationships in education and training.

The assessment criteria are shown in boxes and are followed by questions and activities for you to carry out. Ensure your responses are *specific to you*, the *subject* you will teach and the *context* and *environment* in which you will teach. This unit is at level 3 and therefore does not require academic writing and referencing skills to be demonstrated. The other mandatory units are at level 4.

After completing the activities, check your responses with the second part: **Guidance for evidencing achievement**. This guidance is not intended to give you the answers to questions you may be asked in any formal assessments; however, it will help you focus your responses towards meeting the assessment criteria.

At the end of the chapter is an example of a completed **Assessment grid** which gives ideas for evidence you could provide towards meeting the assessment criteria. Evidence can be cross-referenced between units and assessment criteria if it meets the requirements.

Self-assessment activities

> 2.1 Explain ways to maintain a safe and supportive learning environment

Q8 What do you consider a safe and supportive learning environment to be?

Q9 Explain how you could maintain a safe and supportive learning environment.

> 2.2 Explain why it is important to promote appropriate behaviour and respect for others

Q10 What do you consider to be appropriate behaviour and respect for others?

Q11 Explain why it is important to promote appropriate behaviour and respect for others.

Guidance for evidencing achievement

2.1 Explain ways to maintain a safe and supportive learning environment

Q8 What do you consider a safe and supportive learning environment to be?

Your response could state that all aspects of the learning environment, i.e. physical, social and learning should be appropriate, accessible, supportive, relevant and safe for the subject you will teach and for you and your learners. Informing your learners how you and the organisation will ensure their safety towards each aspect would help make them feel more comfortable and secure, enabling learning to take place. Learners need to know they will be safe when they are with you, and how they won't be faced with any danger. For example, equipment and resources should not cause harm, furniture should not be arranged improperly, heating, lighting and ventilation should be adequate. Safe also relates to learners feeling safe to express their opinions without being ridiculed by others.

Learners should also know that you, their peers and others if necessary, will make their time in the learning environment supportive and productive. Supportive also relates to giving appropriate advice and/or referring your learners to others if you can't help them with something.

Your learners need to know that their safety is of paramount importance to you and your organisation and that everyone (including the learner) has a responsibility for this. This information can be communicated to your learners in various ways, i.e. through staff and learner handbooks, marketing materials, induction procedures, learner contracts, tutorial reviews, and online and learner focus/involvement groups. You might also need to attend safeguarding training to ensure you are up to date with relevant requirements. Safeguarding is a term used to refer to the duties and responsibilities that those providing a health, social or education service have to carry out/perform to protect individuals and vulnerable people from harm.

Your session should always have a clear aim with objectives which your learners know they will be working towards. You should convey how your learners will be supported towards progress and achievement. You should also demonstrate inclusion and challenge any inappropriate or anti-social behaviour as it occurs. Ensuring your learners can have a break, if applicable, and have access to refreshment areas and toilets will help them feel supported in the learning environment.

You should find out what the relevant policies are at your organisation and explain how these will ensure your learners are safe and supported.

Q9 Explain how you could maintain a safe and supportive learning environment.

Your response could explain how the physical, social and learning aspects can impact upon each other, in both positive and negative ways. For example, if the room you are in is too cold, learners might not be able to concentrate, therefore how could you overcome this? If tables are in rows, learners might not be able to communicate well; however, having tables for groups of learners to sit around will enable effective communication. If learners are thirsty or hungry they might not pay attention or could lose concentration. Whilst it is your responsibility to ensure the learning environment is safe and supportive, you might not be able to control some aspects such as heating, lighting or ventilation. However, what you can do is ensure your session is interesting, meaningful and engaging to your learners. This way, your learners will remember more about the session rather than the environment.

Ways of maintaining a supportive learning environment will include negotiating and agreeing ground rules, using appropriate icebreakers, planning your sessions to be inclusive, motivating your learners, encouraging your learners to become actively involved and giving regular guidance, support, praise and feedback. You could encourage peer support through the buddy approach. This enables learners to pair up with someone in the group they feel at ease with. They can then keep in touch with each other between sessions to give encouragement and share support.

You should be aware of the accident, fire and emergency procedures within your organisation. Keeping records such as a register or record of attendance will prove useful should there be a need to evacuate the building – in some organisations it's a legal requirement. The Health and Safety at Work etc. Act (1974) makes it your responsibility to report a hazard if you see it. You would need to take into account your organisation's Health and Safety policy and not do anything outside of your own responsibility, such as moving heavy equipment or asking your learners to work with hazardous materials or dangerous equipment. You might need to carry out risk assessments and some resources, particularly electrical ones, require regular maintenance checks and testing by others. If you see a label on a resource which shows it hasn't been checked for a long time, you will need to report it to the relevant personnel or department.

You could produce a case study of how you have established and maintained a safe and supportive learning environment.

> 2.2 Explain why it is important to promote appropriate behaviour and respect for others

Q10 What do you consider to be appropriate behaviour and respect for others?

Your response could explain that behaviour is all about how you and your learners interact with each other in an acceptable way. Respect is about accepting others, not being rude to them or lowering their confidence and self-esteem in any way. You could explain that you would lead by example to model good practice. If you demonstrate appropriate behaviour and respect for others, hopefully your learners and others will imitate this. As a professional, your role involves acting with integrity, behaving in the correct manner, and respecting others as you would wish them to respect you.

Appropriate behaviour and respect for others includes:

- being honest, reliable and trustworthy

- challenging and managing inappropriate behaviour

- communicating appropriately

- encouraging trust, honesty, politeness and consideration towards others

- ensuring the learning environment is accessible, safe and suitable

- establishing routines

- liaising and working with others in a professional manner

- listening to others' points of view

- negotiating and agreeing ground rules with learners

- not overstepping the boundaries of your role

- planning and preparing adequately

- presenting yourself (for example, the way in which you dress) in a manner which is appropriate to the subject and learning environment

- supporting learners and others as necessary

- treating all learners as individuals

- using a variety of inclusive teaching, learning and assessment approaches

- valuing others' opinions and not imposing your own upon them

Your learners should also demonstrate appropriate behaviour during sessions, and respect their peers and others they come into contact with. This should lead to an appropriate atmosphere in which learning can effectively take place.

Q11 Explain why it is important to promote appropriate behaviour and respect for others.

Your response could explain why you feel it is important, for example, if you didn't challenge and manage inappropriate behaviour, your learners might become disruptive and offensive to you and/or other learners. You could explain what you would do in certain situations, for example, if a colleague did something you believe to be unacceptable, you could have a quiet word with them. However, if it is very serious you might need to report the issue to someone else.

If appropriate behaviour and respect are not established and maintained, disruption could occur and learning might not take place.

You could link your response to your organisation's codes of practice regarding behaviour and respect.

Theory focus

References and further information

Appleyard, N and Appleyard, K (2010) *Communicating with Learners in the Lifelong Learning Sector.* London: Learning Matters SAGE.

Gravells, A (2013) *The Award in Education and Training.* London: Learning Matters SAGE.

Gravells, A and Simpson, S (2014) *The Certificate in Education and Training*. London: Learning Matters SAGE.

National Institute of Adult and Continuing Education (2007) *Safer Practice, Safer Learning*. Ashford: NIACE.

Vizard, D (2012) *How to Manage Behaviour in Further Education*. London: SAGE.

Wallace, S (2007) *Managing Behaviour in the Lifelong Learning Sector* (2nd edn). London: Learning Matters SAGE.

Websites

Behaviour tips – www.pivotaleducation.com

Classroom management free videos – http://www.bestyearever.net/videos/?goback=.gmr_27003.gde_27003_member_196422762

Dealing with behaviour – http://newteachers.tes.co.uk/content/dealing-behaviour-issues-%E2%80%93-guide-new-teachers

Health and Safety at Work etc. Act (1974) – http://www.hse.gov.uk/legislation/hswa.htm

Icebreakers – http://adulted.about.com/od/icebreakerstp/toptenicebreakers.htm and http://www.mwls.co.uk/icebreakers/

Safeguarding – http://www.education.gov.uk/search/results?q=safeguarding

Risk assessments – http://www.hse.gov.uk/risk/fivesteps.htm

Safeguarding Vulnerable Groups Act (2006) – http://www.opsi.gov.uk/ACTS/acts2006/ukpga_20060047_en_1

UNIT TITLE: Understanding roles, responsibilities and relationships in education and training

Assessment grid

Learning Outcomes The learner will:	Assessment Criteria The learner can:		Example evidence
2. Understand ways to maintain a safe and supportive learning environment	2.1	Explain ways to maintain a safe and supportive learning environment	An explanation of what you consider is a safe and supportive learning environment i.e. how you can ensure the physical, social and learning aspects are appropriate, accessible and free from hazards.
			An explanation of how you can maintain a safe and supportive learning environment. For example, carrying out risk assessments.
			Copies of relevant organisational policies and procedures highlighting aspects relating to safety and support for learners.
			Records of risk assessments.
			Records of training attended such as Health and Safety and Safeguarding.
			An anonymised case study of how you have established and maintained a safe and supportive learning environment for your learners.
	2.2	Explain why it is important to promote appropriate behaviour and respect for others	An explanation of what you consider appropriate behaviour and respect for others to be, such as interacting and communicating in an acceptable way.
			An explanation of why it is important to promote appropriate behaviour and respect for others, for example, to create an atmosphere in which learning can effectively take place.
			Written examples of ways you could promote appropriate behaviour and respect for others such as agreeing ground rules, challenging inappropriate behaviour.
			Copies of relevant organisational codes of practice and/or policies highlighting aspects relating to behaviour and respect.

3 UNDERSTAND THE RELATIONSHIPS BETWEEN TEACHERS AND OTHER PROFESSIONALS IN EDUCATION AND TRAINING

This chapter is in two parts. The first part: **Self-assessment activities**, contains questions and activities which relate to the third learning outcome of the Certificate in Education and Training unit Understanding roles, responsibilities and relationships in education and training.

The assessment criteria are shown in boxes and are followed by questions and activities for you to carry out. Ensure your responses are *specific to you*, the *subject* you will teach and the *context* and *environment* in which you will teach. This unit is at level 3 and therefore does not require academic writing and referencing skills to be demonstrated. The other mandatory units are at level 4.

After completing the activities, check your responses with the second part: **Guidance for evidencing achievement**. This guidance is not intended to give you the answers to questions you may be asked in any formal assessments; however, it will help you focus your responses towards meeting the assessment criteria.

At the end of the chapter is an example of a completed **Assessment grid** which gives ideas for evidence you could provide towards meeting the assessment criteria. Evidence can be cross-referenced between units and assessment criteria if it meets the requirements.

Self-assessment activities

> 3.1 Explain how the teaching role involves working with other professionals

Q12 List at least four other professionals (internal and external to your organisation) with whom you might work as part of your teaching role.

Q13 Explain how your role would involve working with the other professionals you have identified in your response to Q12.

> 3.2 Explain the boundaries between the teaching role and other professional roles

Q14 Explain at least four boundaries, which you might encounter between your teaching role and other professional roles.

3.3 Describe points of referral to meet the individual needs of learners

Q15 List at least four individual needs of learners.

Q16 Describe the points of referral to meet the needs you listed in your response to **Q15.**

Guidance for evidencing achievement

3.1 Explain how the teaching role involves working with other professionals

Q12 List at least four other professionals (internal and external to your organisation) with whom you might work as part of your teaching role.

Your response should list at least four other professionals with whom you might work at some point. Your list could include some of the following:

- administration staff
- assessors
- budget holders
- caretakers
- cleaners
- co-tutors
- counsellors
- customers
- external quality assurers
- finance staff
- health and safety officers
- human resources staff
- internal quality assurers

- learning support staff
- managers
- other teachers and trainers
- other training organisations
- probation officers
- reprographics staff
- safeguarding officers
- staff development personnel
- supervisors
- support workers
- technicians
- union staff
- work placement co-ordinators

Q13 Explain how your role would involve working with the other professionals you have identified in your response to Q12.

Your response should explain how you would work with other professionals you have identified in your list. For example:

- Administrative staff – communicating with appropriate personnel to ensure that your learners have been registered with the relevant awarding organisation for a qualification (if applicable). Informing the receptionist of the arrival of visitors so that a visitor's pass, parking and refreshments can be organised.

- External quality assurer – liaising with them regarding changes, for example, to staff and resources, ascertaining details regarding qualification requirements, arranging monitoring dates, providing appropriate information, obtaining feedback and ensuring any action and improvement points are carried out.

- Learning support staff – arranging support for learners with particular needs such as help with maths or using computers.

- Managers – responding to requests for information and data, attending meetings and contributing towards issues under discussion.

It would be useful to find out and understand a little about the job roles of other people you will work with, how they can support you and how you can support them. However, don't feel you need to support them too much by carrying out aspects of their role for them, otherwise you might be blurring the boundary between your role and their role. You should never feel you have to resolve a situation on your own, there should be others who can help when necessary.

You could produce a case study of how your teaching role has involved working with other professionals; however, don't use any names.

3.2 Explain the boundaries between the teaching role and other professional roles

---

Q14 Explain at least four boundaries, which you might encounter between your teaching role and other professional roles.

Your response could explain that boundaries are about knowing where your role as a teacher or trainer stops. You should be able to work within the limits of that role, yet follow all relevant policies and procedures.

Examples include:

- Not doing something which is part of someone else's role. For example, if you need to get handouts photocopied and there is a reprographics department, you shouldn't enter their office and make the copies yourself.

- Not blurring the teaching role with your supportive role, i.e. not becoming too friendly with your learners. For example, you might feel it sensible to make a telephone call to a learner who has been absent but making regular calls would be inappropriate. Giving your personal telephone number to learners could be seen as encouraging informal contact, and you may get calls or texts which are not suitable or relevant. You might not want to take your break with your learners or join their social networking sites as you could become more of a friend than a teacher. When you are with your learners, you need to remain in control, be fair and ethical and not demonstrate any favouritism towards particular learners; for example, by giving one more support than others.

- Not blurring the teaching and assessment roles. For example, you might have taught everything needed for your learners to pass an assignment, but they might not have met the required criteria when answering the questions. You should not pass a learner because you like them, or feel they have worked hard. You must remain objective with your decision and not pass them if they haven't fully met the requirements.

- Not putting your professional role under pressure, for example, accepting a learner on to your programme instead of offering them a more suitable programme, just because you need a certain number of learners for it to go ahead. You might have difficult decisions to make as to whether you accept a learner or not. However, if you make a decision not to accept a learner, it will need to be in the best interests of the learner, and you will need to justify your reasons and keep records.

There are also some common boundaries you should not overstep, i.e. it is unprofessional to use bad language or to let your personal problems affect your work.

You could produce a case study of some boundaries you have encountered between your roles, and how you have overcome them.

3.3 Describe points of referral to meet the individual needs of learners

---

Q15 List at least four individual needs of learners.

Your response should list the individual needs that your learners might have. Your list could include some of the following:

- access to, or fear of, technology

- alcohol or substance misuse

- childcare concerns

- death in the family

- emotional or psychological problems

- English as a second or other language

- financial issues

- health concerns

- limited basic skills such as English and maths

- transport problems

- unsure which career path to take

Q16 Describe the points of referral to meet the needs you listed in your response to Q15.

Your response should describe the points of referral you could recommend to your learners, for those needs you have identified in your list.

For example:

- access to, or fear of technology – local library or internet café, specialist colleagues and/ or training programmes

- alcohol or substance misuse – relevant support agencies, telephone helplines, Citizens Advice Bureau

- health concerns – health centres, general practitioners, hospitals

- unsure which career path to take – National Careers Service, specialist staff within your organisation

You could add the contact details for each, i.e. the names of people, agencies and organisations along with their address, telephone and/or website details.

You could produce a case study regarding the points of referral you have used to meet the individual needs of learners; however, don't use any names of learners.

Theory focus

References and further information

Berry, J (2010) *Teachers' Legal Rights and Responsibilities: A Guide for Trainee Teachers and those New to the Profession* (2nd edn). Hertfordshire: University of Hertfordshire Press.

Gravells, A (2013) *The Award in Education and Training*. London: Learning Matters SAGE.

Gravells, A and Simpson, S (2014) *The Certificate in Education and Training*. London: Learning Matters SAGE.

IfL (2008) *Code of Professional Practice*. London: Institute for Learning.

Tummons, J (2010) *Becoming a Professional Tutor in the Further Education and Skills Sector* (2nd edn). London: Learning Matters SAGE.

Websites

Citizens Advice Bureau – www.citizensadvice.org.uk

Database of self-help groups – www.self-help.org.uk

Dyslexia Association – www.dyslexia.uk.net

National Careers Service – https://nationalcareersservice.direct.gov.uk/Pages/Home.aspx

UNIT TITLE: Understanding roles, responsibilities and relationships in education and training

Assessment grid

Learning Outcomes The learner will:	Assessment Criteria The learner can:		Example evidence
3. Understand the relationships between teachers and other professionals in lifelong learning	3.1	Explain how the teaching role involves working with other professionals	A list of the other professionals with whom you might work as part of your teaching role, such as administration staff, internal quality assurers, learning support staff, managers. An explanation of how your role would involve working with the other professionals you have identified in your list, for example, communicating information. An anonymised case study of how your teaching role has involved working with other professionals.
	3.2	Explain the boundaries between the teaching role and other professional roles	An explanation of the boundaries which you might encounter between your teaching role and your other professional roles, such as not blurring the teaching role with your supportive role, i.e. not becoming too friendly with your learners. An anonymised case study of some boundaries you have encountered between your roles, and how you have overcome them.
	3.3	Describe points of referral to meet the individual needs of learners	A list of individual needs of learners such as childcare concerns, financial issues, limited basic skills, transport problems. A description of relevant points of referral and support systems available such as people, agencies, organisations, websites to meet the needs you have identified. An anonymised case study regarding points of referral you have used to meet the individual needs of learners.

4 BE ABLE TO USE INITIAL AND DIAGNOSTIC ASSESSMENT TO AGREE INDIVIDUAL LEARNING GOALS WITH LEARNERS

This chapter is in two parts. The first part: **Self-assessment activities**, contains questions and activities which relate to the first learning outcome of the Certificate in Education and Training unit Planning to meet the needs of learners in education and training.

The assessment criteria are shown in boxes and are followed by questions and activities for you to carry out. Ensure your responses are *specific to you*, the *subject* you will teach and the *context* and *environment* in which you will teach. As this unit is at level 4, you should use academic writing and referencing when responding to the questions. When referring to a quote, make sure you understand what the quote means and how it will fit within your writing. It could be that you agree with what the author has said and it supports what you are saying, or it could be that you totally disagree with it. If so, explain why you agree or disagree and, if it's the latter, state what you would do differently. You need to write what you think, or what your point of view is, and relate it to your specialist subject.

After completing the activities, check your responses with the second part: **Guidance for evidencing achievement**. This guidance is not intended to give you the answers to questions you may be asked in any formal assessments; however, it will help you focus your responses towards meeting the assessment criteria.

At the end of the chapter is an example of a completed **Assessment grid** which gives ideas for evidence you could provide towards meeting the assessment criteria. Evidence can be cross-referenced between units and assessment criteria if it meets the requirements.

Self-assessment activities

> 1.1 Analyse the role and use of initial and diagnostic assessment in agreeing individual learning goals

Q17 Explain the role of initial and diagnostic assessment.

Q18 Analyse how you could use initial and diagnostic assessment when agreeing individual learning goals.

1.2 Use methods of initial and diagnostic assessment to negotiate and agree individual learning goals with learners

Q19 Demonstrate the use of different methods of initial and diagnostic assessment to negotiate and agree individual goals with learners.

1.3 Record learners' individual learning goals

Q20 Agree individual learning goals with your learners and ensure these are documented.

Guidance for evidencing achievement

1.1 Analyse the role and use of initial and diagnostic assessment in agreeing individual learning goals

Q17 Explain the role of initial and diagnostic assessment.

Your response should explain that it is part of your role to ensure your learners are taking the right programme to enable them to progress towards their chosen career path. Initial and diagnostic assessment is the starting point for finding out about your learner, and matching their needs to the content of the programme or qualification they will be taking. The initial assessment process might be the start of your relationship with your learners. For some learners, this will be an opportunity to divulge any concerns or personal (perhaps confidential) information about themselves.

You could then explain that usually initial assessment takes place at the commencement of your learners' journey, but is effective only when seen as part of a wider and ongoing process. The results can be used to deal with any issues that might arise, or to guide learners to a different, more appropriate programme or level if necessary. You should relate your response to a quote such as 'You will need to be sure that the learner's job, the results of initial assessment, and their aptitudes and attainments indicate that they are likely to succeed in the qualification they have chosen. If you don't do this, you risk setting the learner up for disappointment or failure' (Read, 2011: 26).

It is important to ensure that your learners are on an appropriate or suitable programme, not only for their own benefit, but for your organisation too. It is essential to ascertain if your learner has the appropriate level of experience and knowledge, along with good English, maths, and information and communication technology (ICT) skills. The funding your organisation or learner receives might be affected if they commence, but then leave without achieving.

Your response should reinforce that the role of initial and diagnostic assessment is all about being proactive before learning starts, and active when learning is taking place, rather than being reactive to a situation when it might be too late to do anything. Initial assessment is often referred to as assessment for learning, as the results help inform the learning process. Assessment of learning is about making decisions regarding ongoing progress and achievement. Information gained from these activities will help you plan your sessions to meet any individual needs and/or to arrange further training and support if necessary.

You could then explain what initial and diagnostic assessments can be used for, some of which are listed here:

Initial:

- allow for differentiation and individual requirements to be met
- ascertain why your learner wants to take the programme along with their capability to achieve
- find out the expectations and motivations of your learner

- give your learner the confidence to negotiate and agree individual learning goals

- identify any information which needs to be shared with colleagues

- identify any specific additional support needs or reasonable adjustments which may be required

Diagnostic:

- ascertain learning preferences such as visual, aural, read/write and kinaesthetic (VARK)

- enable learners to demonstrate their current level of skills, knowledge and understanding

- ensure learners can access relevant support such as study skills

- identify an appropriate starting point and level for each learner

- identify gaps in skills, knowledge and understanding to highlight areas to work on

- identify previous experience, knowledge, achievements and transferable skills

- identify specific requirements: for example, English, maths and ICT skills

You could use the diagram shown in Figure 4.1 of the teaching, learning and assessment cycle and annotate on it the role of initial and diagnostic assessment at each stage.

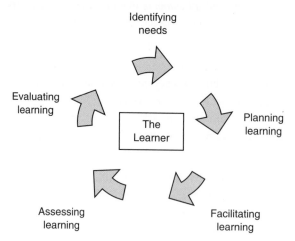

Figure 4.1 The teaching, learning and assessment cycle

Gravells and Simpson, 2014

Q18 Analyse how you could use initial and diagnostic assessment when agreeing individual learning goals.

Your response should be analytical and include points such as the need to try to find out as much as you can about your learners during the initial assessment process. This will give you the opportunity to ensure that the delivery and assessment methods you are planning to use are appropriate for the programme, and will also meet the needs of your learners. You should plan and deliver a range of activities which are based on their learning preferences, so that all your learners feel able to take part at some point in the session.

An important aspect of the initial assessment process is diagnostic assessment. You should use this to evaluate your learner's skills, knowledge, strengths and areas for development for your particular subject area. It could be that your learner feels they are capable of achieving at a higher level than the diagnostic assessments determine. The results will give a thorough indication of not only the level at which your learner needs to be placed for their subject, but also which specific aspects they need to improve on. Skills tests can be used for learners to demonstrate what they can do, knowledge tests can be used for learners to demonstrate their understanding. These results will provide evidence which you can use when negotiating and agreeing individual learning goals.

There are many different types of initial and diagnostic skills tests available that you could use. Some organisations design and use their own, others purchase and use widely available tests, for example, the system called Basic Key Skills Builder (BKSB) to diagnose English, maths and ICT skills. The results of these will give a starting point on which to build your learners' skills. You should relate your response to a quote such as *'At the end of the test the student obtains a printout identifying their level of working and areas that need additional work. Such software frees the teacher from marking and allows them more time to work with the student on improving'* (Reece and Walker, 2007: 361).

You could give an example of an initial or diagnostic assessment activity which you have planned to use with your learners. You can then state how it will help find out your learners' current skills and knowledge, as well as identifying any particular aspects which might otherwise go unnoticed, for example: planning a discussion with your learners regarding their previous achievements and experiences. This could be followed up by a diagnostic assessment, the results of which can be used to confirm (or otherwise) what your learners are telling you. The results could be used to give an indication of not only the level at which your learner needs to be placed for their subject, but also which specific aspects they need to improve on.

You could produce an anonymised case study regarding how you have used different types of initial and diagnostic assessment relevant to your specialist area. You can then analyse how well they worked towards negotiating and agreeing learning goals with a particular individual learner.

> 1.2 Use methods of initial and diagnostic assessment to negotiate and agree individual learning goals with learners

Q19 Demonstrate the use of different methods of initial and diagnostic assessment to negotiate and agree individual goals with learners.

This is a practical task enabling you to demonstrate the use of different methods of initial and diagnostic assessment with your learners, to meet their individual needs. You need to ensure that what you use will be valid and reliable, and that you are being fair and ethical with all your decisions (refer to chapter 13 for more information on using types and methods of assessment).

You should show how the results of initial and diagnostic assessment can be used to help you negotiate appropriate individual learning plans (ILPs) with your learners. This will ensure they are on the right programme at the right level, with the support they need to succeed. Initial assessment results should not be filed away and then never referred to or used again. They should be continually accessed to ensure you are familiar with each learner and their needs.

Examples could include a visual (i.e. a picture, drawing or timeline) of a learner journey highlighting where initial and diagnostic assessments have had an impact, for example, where a learner has had to make alterations to their original learning goals.

You could also include copies of anonymised initial and diagnostic assessment activities which you have used and are relevant to your subject area. Examples include:

- application/enrolment forms: to show what questions are asked

- interview/discussion notes: asking your learner why they are there, what they want to achieve and discussing their learning history and preferred style of learning

- observations: it may be necessary to observe your learner performing a skill, perhaps in their workplace, before agreeing an appropriate programme and level

- self-assessment: asking your learner to assess their own skills and knowledge towards the programme outcomes. This is often known as a skills scan

- structured activities: for example, role play

- tests: for example, literacy, language, numeracy and ICT. These can be a hardcopy or online via the internet or your organisation's intranet.

You should keep evidence of what you have used to show your assessor, who might also observe you with your learners. Be prepared to justify all your decisions.

Evidence could include anonymised initial assessment records, copies of written initial assessment questionnaires, discussion notes and diagnostic test results.

1.3 Record learners' individual learning goals

Q20 Agree individual learning goals with your learners and ensure these are documented.

This is a practical task enabling you to agree individual learning goals with your learners. Records must be maintained to satisfy your organisation's internal quality assurance systems, and external regulators such as Ofsted, as well as awarding organisations if the qualifications are accredited. They will expect to see differentiated progress records for each of your learners, identical ILPs for each of your learners will not be acceptable. The records will need to show that each learner has had an opportunity to be involved in agreeing their own learning experience.

You could provide evidence of an anonymised ILP which demonstrates that the process of negotiating and agreeing individual learning goals has been revisited many times during a learner's programme. It is important to show that negotiation and agreement of learning goals can happen during any of the stages of the teaching, learning and assessment cycle, i.e. identifying needs, planning, facilitating, assessing and evaluating. You must keep in mind the requirements of the programme as a key part of your discussions with learners. This will ensure that they can achieve what they are expected to by the agreed dates. The purpose of negotiating and agreeing individual goals is to find out how your learner is going to work towards achieving them.

You could make a video of you discussing and agreeing individual learning goals with a learner; just make sure you obtain the relevant permissions.

Theory focus

References and further information

Farrell, M (2006) *Dyslexia and Other Learning Difficulties.* London: Routledge.

Gravells, A (2013) *The Award in Education and Training.* London: Learning Matters SAGE.

Gravells, A and Simpson, S (2014) *The Certificate in Education and Training.* London: Learning Matters SAGE.

Gravells, A and Simpson, S (2012) *Equality and Diversity in the Lifelong Learning Sector* (2nd edn). London: Learning Matters SAGE.

Peart, S and Atkins, L (2011) *Teaching 14–19 Learners in the Lifelong Learning Sector.* London: Learning Matters SAGE.

Powell, S and Tummons, J (2011) *Inclusive Practice in the Lifelong Learning Sector.* London: Learning Matters SAGE.

Read, H (2011) *The Best Assessor's Guide.* Bideford: Read On Publications Ltd.

Reece, I and Walker, S (2007) *Teaching, Training and Learning: A Practical Guide* (6th edn). Tyne & Wear: Business Education Publishers.

Wallace, S (2011) *Teaching, Tutoring and Training in the Lifelong Learning Sector* (4th edn). London: Learning Matters SAGE.

Websites

Inclusion, equality, diversity and differentiation resources – http://reflect.ifl.ac.uk/viewasset.aspx?oid=3 201642&type=webfolio&pageoid=3201743

Inclusive teaching resources, weblinks and videos – http://www.open.ac.uk/inclusiveteaching/pages/ general/a-z.php

Initial and diagnostic assessment – http://archive.excellencegateway.org.uk/page.aspx?o=BSFAlearning difficulty%2Finitialassess

Open University inclusive teaching – www.open.ac.uk/inclusiveteaching/pages/inclusive-teaching/ index.php

UNIT TITLE: Planning to meet the needs of learners in education and training

Assessment grid

Learning Outcomes The learner will:	Assessment Criteria The learner can:		Example evidence
1. Be able to use initial and diagnostic assessment to agree individual learning goals with learners	1.1	Analyse the role and use of initial and diagnostic assessment in agreeing individual learning goals	An explanation of the role of initial and diagnostic assessment, i.e. to ascertain information relating to each learner to ensure they are on the right programme at the right level. An analysis of how the results of initial and diagnostic assessments can be used to agree individual learning goals, i.e. what will be used, why and how. An anonymised case study analysing how you have used initial and diagnostic assessment with your learners. An annotated diagram of the teaching, learning and assessment cycle explaining the role of initial and diagnostic assessment at each stage.
	1.2	Use methods of initial and diagnostic assessment to negotiate and agree individual learning goals with learners	Evidence of using initial and diagnostic assessment activities relevant to your subject area such as anonymised documents and records which have been used with learners, for example, application/enrolment forms, interview/discussion notes, observations, self-assessment activities, skills tests. A visual (i.e. a picture, drawing or timeline) of a learner journey highlighting where initial and diagnostic assessments results have been used to make alterations to their original learning goals. Your assessor's observation report and feedback, along with records of any discussions.
	1.3	Record learners' individual learning goals	Evidence of recording learner involvement in the negotiation and agreement of their learning goals such as anonymised completed ILPs. An anonymised tutorial record showing initial learning goals agreed, a change in circumstances then renegotiated learning goals and additional support agreed. A visual or audio recording of you discussing and agreeing individual learning goals with a learner (with relevant permissions). Your assessor's observation report and feedback, along with records of any discussions.

5 BE ABLE TO PLAN INCLUSIVE TEACHING AND LEARNING IN ACCORDANCE WITH INTERNAL AND EXTERNAL REQUIREMENTS

This chapter is in two parts. The first part: **Self-assessment activities**, contains questions and activities which relate to the second learning outcome of the Certificate in Education and Training unit Planning to meet the needs of learners in education and training.

The assessment criteria are shown in boxes and are followed by questions and activities for you to carry out. Ensure your responses are *specific to you*, the *subject* you will teach and the *context* and *environment* in which you will teach. As this unit is at level 4, you should use academic writing and referencing when responding to the questions. When referring to a quote, make sure you understand what the quote means and how it will fit within your writing. It could be that you agree with what the author has said and it supports what you are saying, or it could be that you totally disagree with it. If so, explain why you agree or disagree and, if it's the latter, state what you would do differently. You need to write what you think, or what your point of view is, and relate it to your specialist subject.

After completing the activities, check your responses with the second part: **Guidance for evidencing achievement**. This guidance is not intended to give you the answers to questions you may be asked in any formal assessments; however, it will help you focus your responses towards meeting the assessment criteria.

At the end of the chapter is an example of a completed **Assessment grid** which gives ideas for evidence you could provide towards meeting the assessment criteria. Evidence can be cross-referenced between units and assessment criteria if it meets the requirements.

Self-assessment activities

2.1 Devise a scheme of work in accordance with internal and external requirements

Q21 What information would you need to be able to devise a scheme of work in accordance with internal and external requirements?

Q22 Devise a scheme of work for your specialist subject which meets internal and external requirements. Internal requirements might include embedding English, maths and information and communication technology (ICT). External requirements will include those imposed by awarding and regulatory organisations.

> 2.2 Design teaching and learning plans that meet the aims and individual needs of all learners and curriculum requirements

Q23 Referring to your scheme of work, design teaching and learning plans (often referred to as session plans) for at least the first four sessions. Ensure your plans meet the aims and individual needs of all your learners, as well as the curriculum requirements.

> 2.3 Explain how own planning meets the individual needs of learners

Q24 Explain how the planning process, for example, using your scheme of work and teaching and learning plans, can meet the needs of individual learners.

> 2.4 Explain ways in which teaching and learning plans can be adapted to meet the individual needs of learners

Q25 Explain how you would adapt teaching and learning plans to meet the individual needs of learners.

> 2.5 Identify opportunities for learners to provide feedback to inform inclusive practice

Q26 What does the term inclusive practice mean?

Q27 What opportunities can you identify for learners to provide feedback?

Q28 How can you use this feedback to inform inclusive practice?

Guidance for evidencing achievement

2.1 Devise a scheme of work in accordance with internal and external requirements

---

Q21 What information would you need to be able to devise a scheme of work in accordance with internal and external requirements?

Your response should state that you will need to know the details of the programme or qualification and the groups of individual learners you will be teaching to devise your scheme of work. You will need to prepare one whether you teach groups or individuals; however you may need to explain that the format required is likely to be different. The scheme of work will help you plan what you will do and when, along with what resources you will need and when, and give you an idea of what you need to prepare in advance.

Your response could include an explanation of internal and external requirements. For example, internal: embedding functional skills within each session; external: following the assessment criteria of the qualification which is accredited by an awarding organisation.

You could include an example of a scheme of work which is currently used within your organisation and will show the information you need to devise the content.

You could include in your response the 'five Ws and one H' rationale to help you gather the information you need, i.e.:

- who the sessions are for, i.e. the individuals in your groups (who)

- what you want your learners to achieve, i.e. any learning support resources (what)

- the number of sessions, dates and times (when)

- venue or environment (where)

- the objectives or learning outcomes of the programme or qualification (why)

- teaching and learning approaches, resources and assessment methods (how)

You could produce a detailed group profile before composing your scheme of work which will show that you have considered your learners as individuals. A group profile is a detailed list of your learners along with information such as prior achievement, learning preferences, needs and targets.

You should relate your response to a range of relevant legislation that may have an impact on you and your learners when devising your scheme of work. For example, the Equality Act (2010), and the Health and Safety at Work etc. Act (1974). You will need to be aware of any updates that will need to be considered when you are devising your scheme of work.

Q22 Devise a scheme of work for your specialist subject which meets internal and external requirements. Internal requirements might include embedding English, maths and information and communication technology (ICT). External requirements will include those imposed by awarding and regulatory organisations.

This is a practical task enabling you to devise a scheme of work for your specialist subject which meets internal and external requirements. Ideally, it should be for four sessions or more.

You should keep evidence of what you have done to show your assessor, who might also observe you with your learners. Be prepared to justify all your decisions.

Evidence could include different types of schemes of work for your specialist subject area, i.e. one which is appropriate for a group and one which is appropriate for an individual, documents from the relevant awarding organisation showing evidence of the learning outcomes and assessment criteria to be covered. Evidence should show your planning has been differentiated to meet the needs of your learners.

> 2.2 Design teaching and learning plans that meet the aims and individual needs of all learners and curriculum requirements

Q23 Referring to your scheme of work, design teaching and learning plans (often referred to as session plans) for at least the first four sessions. Ensure your plans meet the aims and individual needs of all your learners, as well as the curriculum requirements.

This is a practical task enabling you to design your teaching and learning plans (also known as session plans) for at least the first four sessions. Your teaching and learning plans should be fit for purpose in such a way that the learning taking place is set in a realistic context for the programme and/or qualification, whilst meeting the individual needs of your learners. Any internal or external observer should be able to look at your teaching and learning plan and know what you want your learners to achieve during your session.

Your teaching and learning plans are an extension of your scheme of work and you should always refer back to it when designing your plans. It is important that there is collaboration between the two planning documents, i.e. your scheme of work gives the high-level information about your programme and your teaching and learning plans give the finer details for each session. This approach should be used whether you are teaching a group or individuals, although the way in which the information is documented may be different. Your teaching and learning plans should include details such as:

- the date, time, duration, venue, number of learners

- a clear aim of what you want your learners to achieve

- the context of the session, for example, references to the qualification being delivered

- a group profile, for example, age, prior experience, particular needs, learning preferences, behaviour concerns

- realistic objectives or learning outcomes at an appropriate level for your learners (you might be required to differentiate these into what you expect all, most and some of your learners to achieve)

- teaching, learning and assessment activities with allocated timings (be prepared to be flexible)

- resources to be used

- available learner support and how it is to be used (for example, you might have access to volunteers to support your learners)

You should keep evidence of what you have done to show your assessor, who might also observe you with your learners. Be prepared to justify all your decisions.

Evidence could include different types of teaching and learning plans for your specialist subject area, i.e. one which is appropriate for a group and one which is appropriate for an individual, documents from the relevant awarding organisation showing evidence of the learning outcomes and assessment criteria to be met. Evidence should show your planning has been differentiated to meet the needs of your learners.

2.3 Explain how own planning meets the individual needs of learners

---

Q24 Explain how the planning process, for example, using your scheme of work and teaching and learning plans, can meet the needs of individual learners.

Your response should explain that exploring how you can meet the needs of your individual learners is one of the main tasks in the planning process. Your scheme of work and teaching and learning plans should naturally develop and grow from this exploration.

Your response could explain that during the planning process you have considered the key principles of adult learning based on Knowles et al. (2005). This will have had an impact on the way in which you design your scheme of work and teaching and learning plans. Your planning should allow time early on in the programme to obtain details regarding your learners' individual needs. You should also find out and incorporate your learners' experiences and knowledge which is relevant to the subject topic. You should include your learners' experiences and knowledge whenever you can to build on what they already know and can do.

One of Knowles et al.'s (2005) key principles for successful adult learning is that adults have built up diverse life experiences and knowledge that may include work-related activities, family responsibilities and previous education experiences. They need to be able to connect their new learning to existing learning. Your response could give an anonymised example of how you have found out information about a learner in the early stages of your programme and how you have used the information in your planning to meet their needs.

Your response should include an example of the approach you have taken to ensure your documents meet the programme requirements and the individual needs of your learners. Your documents should:

- have a beginning, middle and end to each session

- be structured and logical

- be based on learning preferences, for example, visual, aural, read/write and kinaesthetic (VARK)

- show any individual learning needs and support required

- contain activities that link to real work experiences and current skills and knowledge

- demonstrate how you will engage and motivate your learners by varying the teaching, learning and assessment activities

- show a contingency plan in case something doesn't work or the timings change

- reflect the use of new technology where possible

You could relate your response to a quote from Fleming (2005), who stated that people can be grouped into four styles of learning: visual, aural, read/write and kinaesthetic, known by the acronym VARK. However, not all learners fall into just one style as they may be multi-modal, i.e. a mixture of two or more preferences enabling learning to take place more quickly. You could note in your plan what you think the learning style is of each of the activities you have planned to use. This will help you check that your plan captures a range of styles in each session. You might be required to embed the functional skills of English, maths and ICT during your sessions and this could also be noted. When planning you will need to ensure that any activities are realistic and relevant to enable your learners to engage with real situations in their subject area.

You could produce an anonymised case study regarding how you have planned a scheme of work and subsequent teaching and learning plans for a particular programme or qualification.

2.4 Explain ways in which teaching and learning plans can be adapted to meet the individual needs of learners

---

Q25 Explain how you would adapt teaching and learning plans to meet the individual needs of learners.

Your response should recognise that each learner on your programme will learn in a different way and at a different pace. This means that you will need to adapt your teaching and learning plans to meet the differing needs of your learners. You should therefore use varied approaches to reach all learning preferences. What works with one learner or group might not work well with others, perhaps due to their learning preferences or other influences. However, don't change something for the sake of it; if it works, hopefully it will continue to work.

You could relate your response to the report of Professor Frank Coffield of the University of London who carried out a systematic and critical review of learning preferences in 2004 in post-16 learning. Coffield later states 'it was not sufficient to pay attention to individual differences in learners, we must take account of the whole teaching–learning environment' (2008: 31). It is important that your learners are challenged further and this may mean helping them to explore other ways in which they think they learn.

Your response could explain that you should review the effectiveness of your own teaching to enable you to develop and improve further. The process should also take into account the views of your learners and others with whom you come into contact. Reviewing your practice will help you identify any problems or concerns, enabling you to do things differently next time. Never assume everything is going well just because you think it is. Don't be put off adapting your teaching and learning plans to try something new because you may have tried something in the past that hasn't worked. Learning occurs for everyone involved in the teaching and learning process and that means you too.

Your response should explain that your teaching and learning plans can be adapted at any time, i.e. you may need to adapt them during a session. This could be as a result of an activity not going as you originally planned. As soon as possible after the session, you should carry out a self-evaluation and reflect on how it went. Make notes of any changes you would make that could help you if you were to deliver this same session again. Also consider whether or not you need to address any gaps in your own skills and knowledge and make sure you do something about it. The most effective and convincing plans are those where it can be seen that they are working documents, for example, you've scribbled notes on your plan about something you need to change.

Your response could state an example of an evaluation you have carried out which has resulted in an adaptation to your plans. However, if you have planned ahead too far, a change in one of your teaching and learning plans may have an impact on the others too.

2.5 Identify opportunities for learners to provide feedback to inform inclusive practice

---

Q26 What does the term inclusive practice mean?

Your response should explain that inclusive practice means ensuring a match between each individual's requirements and the provision that is made for them. Your organisation may have a learner entitlement statement which will reflect learners' individual circumstances and needs. The statement should take into account the needs of particular groups, such as those with learning difficulties or disabilities, a visual or hearing impairment, those whose first language is not English and/or those who require support with their English, maths or ICT skills. It should therefore encourage equality of opportunity for all learners.

To promote inclusive practice effectively for all learners, there is a need to bring equality, diversity and rights issues into the mainstream, to ensure they are no longer viewed as something affecting only minority groups. Those affected by stereotyping, prejudice and discrimination are not always in the minority and you should be careful not to indulge the minority at the expense of the majority.

You could produce an anonymised case study regarding a group of learners from different backgrounds and cultures, and/or with different needs and abilities and state how these have been met. This could demonstrate that inclusive practice adds value to your teaching by recognising the many differences your learners have, and incorporating their diverse experiences into your sessions.

Q27 What opportunities can you identify for learners to provide feedback?

Your response should identify that it is important that your learners have an opportunity to give feedback on their learning experiences. Ofsted describes this *as the learner voice.* This is the involvement of learners and potential learners in shaping the learning opportunities that are available to them. It means involving and supporting them to act as partners with policy makers, providers, practitioners and other agencies. Learner voice initiatives seek to include the learner by enabling them to express their concerns, needs and views, in a safe way. Your learners need to have this opportunity at all stages of their learning programme, not just at the end when it may be too late to make any changes.

Your response could identify some ways learners can provide their feedback. For example:

- the use of anonymous questionnaires

- the use of online surveys and polls

- talking to your learners informally during tutorial reviews, at break times, or before or after your sessions

- learners writing comments on a post-it note and sticking it on a flipchart or wall for you to gather at the end of the session

- facilitating the development of a learner forum

- learners voting for two or three other learners to represent the group at relevant meetings

Your response should state that there should always be opportunities to build in time during your session for your learners to give feedback. Make sure you analyse the feedback and inform your learners how their contributions have led to changes and improvements.

Q28 How can you use this feedback to inform inclusive practice?

Your response should show how you can use feedback from your learners to help improve the learning environment and their learning experience. Your learners are the best judges of whether they are getting what they feel they need. If given the opportunity, they may give you more feedback in an informal situation such as a discussion, rather than a formal situation such as completing a survey.

You could create a list of opportunities where your learners could give feedback to both you and your organisation that will inform inclusive practice. This could be promoted to your learners during their induction to your programme which will highlight that there is a culture that learners are at the heart of your organisation's work. An example could be a calendar of events where learners are consulted about changes the organisation is propos-ing to make. However, if your organisation is serious about responding appropriately to the issues that are raised, and gives feedback as to developments and changes as a result, then learners should be consulted in all aspects of the decision-making process. As a result, your learners are more likely to make the necessary commitment to learning and to be success-ful in achieving their goals.

Evaluation and feedback can contribute to your organisation's quality assurance process by helping improve the service given to learners, not only during sessions, but in other aspects such as the facilities which are available.

You should keep evidence of what you have done to show your assessor, who might also observe you with your learners. Be prepared to justify all your decisions.

Theory focus

References and further information

Coffield, F (2004) *Learning Preferences and Pedagogy in Post-16 Learning*. London: Learning and Skills Research Centre.

Coffield, F (2008) *Just Suppose Teaching and Learning Became the First Priority*. London: Learning and Skills Network.

Fleming, N (2005) *VARK – A Guide to Learning Styles*. Available at http://www.vark-learn.com/english/index.asp (accessed 02.03.14).

Gravells, A and Simpson, S (2014) *The Certificate in Education and Training*. London: Learning Matters SAGE.

Honey, P and Mumford, A (2000) *The Learning Preferences Helper's Guide*. Coventry: Peter Honey Publications.

Knowles, M S, Elwood, F H III and Swanson, R A (2005) *The Adult Learner*. Oxford: Butterworth-Heinemann.

Peart, S and Atkins, L (2011) *Teaching 14–19 Learners in the Lifelong Learning Sector*. London: Learning Matters SAGE.

Petty, G (2009) *Teaching Today: A Practical Guide*. Cheltenham: Nelson Thornes.

Rogers, A and Horrocks, N (2010) *Teaching Adults* (4th edn). Maidenhead: OU Press.

Websites

Equality Act (2010) – http://www.legislation.gov.uk/ukpga/2010/15/contents

Equality and Diversity Forum – www.edf.org.uk

Learning preference questionnaire – www.vark-learn.com

Learning theories – www.learning-theories.com

Functional skills – http://www.qca.org.uk/qca_6062.aspx

Ofsted – ofsted.gov.uk

Online presentations – www.prezi.com

Teaching and learning theories – http://classweb.gmu.edu/ndabbagh/Resources/IDKB/models_theories.htm

Teacher training videos for using ICT – www.teachertrainingvideos.com/latest.html

Theories of learning – www.learningandteaching.info/learning/

Tips for teaching adults – http://www.helium.com/knowledge/61278-tips-for-teaching-adult-learners-instead-of-younger-learners

UNIT TITLE: Planning to meet the needs of learners in education and training

Assessment grid

Learning Outcomes The learner will:	Assessment Criteria The learner can:		Example evidence
2. Be able to plan inclusive teaching and learning in accordance with internal and external requirements	2.1	Devise a scheme of work in accordance with internal and external requirements	An explanation of the information required to be able to devise a scheme of work in accordance with internal and external requirements.
			A detailed group profile to show that you have considered your learners as individuals and how you are planning to support them.
			An identification of a range of relevant legislation that may have an impact on planning, such as the Equality Act (2010), the Health and Safety at Work etc. Act (1974).
			A completed scheme of work for your specialist subject.
			Your assessor's observation report and feedback, along with records of any discussions.
	2.2	Design teaching and learning plans that meet the aims and individual needs of all learners and curriculum requirements	Teaching and learning plans relevant to your subject area which are differentiated to meet the needs of your learners.
			Evidence of documents from the relevant awarding organisations showing the learning outcomes and assessment criteria covered by your teaching and learning plans.
			Your assessor's observation report and feedback, along with records of any discussions.
	2.3	Explain how own planning meets the individual needs of learners	Evidence of how you have obtained details regarding your individual learners in the early stages of the programme and how you have used it in your planning.
			An anonymised case study regarding devising schemes of work and teaching and learning plans for a particular programme or qualification.
			Your assessor's observation report and feedback, along with records of any discussions.
	2.4	Explain ways in which teaching and learning plans can be adapted to meet the individual needs of learners	Evidence of evaluation regarding planning, and subsequent adaptations to your teaching and learning plans.
			An explanation of how you could adapt your teaching and learning plans to meet the individual needs of your learners.
			Your assessor's observation report and feedback, along with records of any discussions.
	2.5	Identify opportunities for learners to provide feedback to inform inclusive practice	A list of potential opportunities for your learners to provide feedback within your organisation, for example, questionnaires and surveys.
			Evidence of your organisation's learner entitlement statement setting out what is expected from learners and what they can expect from the organisation (if applicable).
			An anonymised case study showing how you have met the needs of learners from different backgrounds and cultures, to demonstrate inclusive practice.
			A calendar of events informing learners where and when there are opportunities for them to provide feedback to inform inclusive practice.
			Your assessor's observation report and feedback, along with records of any discussions.

6 BE ABLE TO IMPLEMENT THE MINIMUM CORE IN PLANNING INCLUSIVE TEACHING AND LEARNING

This chapter is in two parts. The first part: **Self-assessment activities**, contains questions and activities which relate to the third learning outcome of the Certificate in Education and Training unit Planning to meet the needs of learners in education and training.

The assessment criteria are shown in boxes and are followed by questions and activities for you to carry out. Ensure your responses are *specific to you*, the *subject* you will teach and the *context* and *environment* in which you will teach. As this unit is at level 4, you should use academic writing and referencing when responding to the questions. When referring to a quote, make sure you understand what the quote means and how it will fit within your writing. It could be that you agree with what the author has said and it supports what you are saying, or it could be that you totally disagree with it. If so, explain why you agree or disagree and, if it's the latter, state what you would do differently. You need to write what you think, or what your point of view is, and relate it to your specialist subject.

After completing the activities, check your responses with the second part: **Guidance for evidencing achievement**. This guidance is not intended to give you the answers to questions you may be asked in any formal assessments; however, it will help you focus your responses towards meeting the assessment criteria.

At the end of the chapter is an example of a completed **Assessment grid** which gives ideas for evidence you could provide towards meeting the assessment criteria. Evidence can be cross-referenced between units and assessment criteria if it meets the requirements.

Self-assessment activities

> 3.1 Analyse ways in which minimum core elements can be demonstrated in planning inclusive teaching and learning

Q29 What is the minimum core?

Q30 Analyse how you can demonstrate minimum core elements when planning inclusive learning.

> 3.2 Apply minimum core elements in planning inclusive teaching and learning

Q31 Demonstrate how you can apply the relevant minimum core elements when planning inclusive teaching and learning.

Guidance for evidencing achievement

> 3.1 Analyse ways in which minimum core elements can be demonstrated in planning inclusive teaching and learning

Q29 What is the minimum core?

Your response should state that the minimum core consists of four elements which are literacy, language, numeracy and information and communication technology (ICT). These elements should be demonstrated as part of your teaching role.

The minimum core aims to:

- promote an understanding that underpinning literacy, language, numeracy and ICT skills may be needed for learners to succeed and achieve their chosen qualification

- encourage the development of inclusive practices to addressing the literacy, language, numeracy and ICT needs of learners

- raise awareness of the benefits to learners of developing embedded approaches to teaching, learning and assessment of English, maths and ICT

- provide signposts to useful materials which will support collaborative working with specialist teachers of literacy, language, numeracy and ICT in understanding how to integrate these skills within other areas of specialism (LLUK, 2007: 6)

You should develop and demonstrate your skills of literacy, language, numeracy and ICT to at least level 2. This will enable you to support your learners with English, maths and ICT (known as functional skills). It will also ensure you teach your area of specialism as effectively as possible.

You should relate your response to a quote such as: *'The introduction of the minimum core will provide a foundation upon which all teachers can develop their own skills as well as their ability to identify when it is appropriate to work with subject specialists'* (LSIS, 2007 [revised 2013]: 4).

You could state that you are not expected to be a specialist teacher of English, maths and ICT but that you should have the knowledge and skills required in the minimum core elements. There will be many naturally occurring activities during sessions for developing these skills for yourself and your learners.

Q30 Analyse how you can demonstrate minimum core elements when planning inclusive learning.

Your response should analyse how you can demonstrate the different minimum core elements, i.e. literacy, language, numeracy and information and communication technology (ICT), when planning inclusive learning. For example:

Literacy

Reading and annotating the qualification guidance to ascertain what the requirements are for your subject. Analysing and interpreting the programme or qualification requirements to devise a scheme of work and teaching and learning plans. Plans need to be unambiguous and clearly written: differentiating activities and resources to meet the needs of individual learners, checking spelling, grammar, punctuation and syntax of all documents created before issuing them to learners.

You should relate your response to a quote such as: *'Differentiating schemes of work and lesson plans will meet the individual needs, aims and experiences of learners'* (Skills for Business, 2007: 27).

Language

Explaining initial and diagnostic assessment activities to learners. Using clear language when giving instructions both spoken and written, at an appropriate level. Avoiding the use of jargon wherever possible and explaining acronyms and abbreviations. Offering opportunities for learners to have one-to-one tutorials to discuss arrangements for meeting their individual needs and how any special arrangements will work within the group and the learning environment. Asking questions to check a learner's knowledge and understanding and listening to their responses. Listening to questions and answering them appropriately. Constructing logical and realistic individual learning plans.

You should relate your response to a quote such as: *'Acronyms and jargon are ways of excluding people by talking in a way where only some people know what is being said ... we need to use inclusive language that everyone can understand'* (Friedman, 2009: Kindle 9%).

Numeracy

Calculating how long various activities will take, which might be complex if you are planning a range of differentiated activities at different levels. Monitoring how long learners are taking to carry out an activity, and what time they have left to complete it. Evaluating how this is impacting on the timing in your planning, for example, if an activity is taking longer than you planned, do you need to alter timings for the rest of the session and if so, by how much?

Breaking down the overall number of hours for your programme into an appropriate timeframe for delivery and achievement, i.e. the number of weeks, number of sessions, number of activities. Calculating how long it will take to devise various aspects of the planning process, for example, how long will initial assessments take and will you need to adjust this based on any differing individual requirements?

You should relate your response to a quote such as: *'As the world of work has changed, so have demands on employees. In advanced economies there is now an increasing need for employees to have a higher level of skills in all areas, including number'* (Peart, 2009: 69).

ICT

Creating and adapting promotional materials relevant to your programme, for example, information leaflets. Preparing online initial assessment materials, uploading documents to a virtual learning environment (VLE) or other system. Using a word processor or other application to record the results of your learners' initial and diagnostic assessments, for example, producing and updating an electronic ILP. Using email or social networking to communicate appropriately. Using an electronic registration system to record your learners' attendance. Using the internet for research purposes, for example, ascertaining updates to relevant legislation, finding information about a particular topic you have planned to deliver.

Using new technology for activities such as an online enrolment, welcome surveys and completing learning preference questionnaires. Using digital media for visual/audio recording and playback of initial assessment activities.

You should relate your response to a quote such as: '*Your professional reputation is clearly valuable to your current and future career and consequentially managing your online reputation is an essential part of being a teacher*' (Childnet International 2011, accessed 11 August 2013).

3.2 Apply minimum core elements in planning inclusive teaching and learning

---

Q31 Demonstrate how you can apply the relevant minimum core elements when planning inclusive teaching and learning.

This is a practical task enabling you to use the minimum core elements you have analysed in Q30.

You should keep evidence of what you have done to show your assessor, who might also observe you with your learners. Be prepared to justify all your decisions.

Evidence could include:

Literacy

- individual learning plans
- initial and diagnostic assessment activities and materials such as skills scans, English and maths tests, or questions regarding learning difficulties or disabilities
- scheme of work
- teaching and learning plans (session plans)
- tutorial review records

Language

- a visual or digital recording of you speaking to your learners and responding to their questions (with their permission)
- an induction presentation you have created to enable learners' understanding of the programme or qualification requirements

Numeracy

- a statistical analysis of data received from surveys
- an analysis of retention and achievement targets compared to previous years
- an analysis of skills scans results
- an evaluation of initial and diagnostic assessment results

ICT

- a visual recording of you using technology which you have adapted to meet the needs of your learners, for example, uploading materials, communicating, negotiating work activities and agreeing deadlines

- audio, digital and electronic materials and records

- emails

- online communications, polls and surveys

- online learning preference questionnaire results and how they inform the planning process

You could produce an anonymous case study of how you have applied the minimum core elements when planning teaching and learning.

Theory focus

References and further information

Appleyard, N and Appleyard, K (2009) *The Minimum Core for Language and Literacy*. London: Learning Matters SAGE.

Clark, A (2009) *The Minimum Core for Information and Communication Technology*. London: Learning Matters SAGE.

Coffield, F (2008) *Just Suppose Teaching and Learning Became the First Priority*. London: Learning and Skills Network.

Friedman, M (2009) *Trying Hard Is Not Good Enough*. Santa Fe, NM: FPSI Publishing (Kindle version).

Gravells, A and Simpson, S (2014) *The Certificate in Education and Training*. London: Learning Matters SAGE.

LLUK (2007) *Literacy, Language, Numeracy and ICT: Inclusive Learning Approaches for all Teachers, Tutors and Trainers in the Learning and Skills Sector*. London: Lifelong Learning UK.

LSIS (2007, revised 2013) *Addressing Literacy, Language, Numeracy and ICT Needs in Education and Training: Defining the Minimum Core of Teachers' Knowledge, Understanding and Personal Skills – A Guide for Initial Teacher Education Programmes*. Coventry: LSIS.

Peart, S (2009) *The Minimum Core for Numeracy*. London: Learning Matters SAGE.

Skills for Business (2007) *Inclusive Learning Approaches for Literacy, Language, Numeracy and ICT: Companion Guide to the Minimum Core*. Nottingham: DfES Publications.

Websites

Assessment tools (literacy, numeracy, ESOL, dyslexia) – www.excellencegateway.org.uk/toolslibrary

Approved literacy and numeracy qualifications – http://www.ifl.ac.uk/__data/assets/pdf_file/0006/27753/Level-2-Literacy-and-Numeracy-Skills-_June-2012.pdf

Childnet International – www.childnet.com/resources/social-networking-a-guide-for-teachers-and-professionals

Computer free support – www.onlinebasics.co.uk and http://learn.go-on.co.uk

Digital Unite – http://digitalunite.com/guides

Digital technologies for education and research – www.jisc.ac.uk

English and maths free support – www.move-on.org.uk

Functional skills criteria – http://www2.ofqual.gov.uk/downloads/category/68-functional-skills-subject-criteria

Initial assessment tools – www.toolslibrary.co.uk

Minimum Core Standards – http://repository.excellencegateway.org.uk/fedora/objects/import-pdf:93/datastreams/PDF/content

Minimum Core – inclusive learning approaches for literacy, language, numeracy and ICT (2007) – http://www.excellencegateway.org.uk/node/12020

UNIT TITLE: Planning to meet the needs of learners in education and training

Assessment grid

Learning Outcomes The learner will:	Assessment Criteria The learner can:	Example evidence
3. Be able to implement the minimum core in planning inclusive teaching and learning	3.1 Analyse ways in which minimum core elements can be demonstrated in planning inclusive teaching and learning	An explanation of what the minimum core is, for example, the four elements of literacy, language, numeracy and information and communication technology (ICT) which should be demonstrated by all teachers to at least level 2. A written analysis of ways in which you can demonstrate the different minimum core elements, for example: *Literacy:* analysing and interpreting the qualification requirements to create a scheme of work and teaching and learning plans. *Language:* planning the clear use of language in giving instructions both spoken and written at an appropriate level in your teaching, learning and assessment plans. *Numeracy:* breaking down the overall number of hours for your programme into an appropriate timeframe for delivery and achievement, i.e. number of weeks, number of sessions, number of activities. *ICT:* using the internet for research purposes, for example, updates to relevant legislation, knowledge about a particular topic.
	3.2 Apply minimum core elements in planning inclusive teaching and learning	Anonymised evidence of using the different minimum core elements when planning inclusive teaching and learning such as: *Literacy* • individual learning plans • initial and diagnostic assessment activities and materials such as skills scans, English and maths tests, or questions regarding learning difficulties or disabilities • scheme of work • teaching and learning plans (session plans) • tutorial review records. *Language* • a visual or digital recording of you speaking to your learners and responding to their questions (with their permission) • an induction presentation you have created to enable learners' understanding of the programme or qualification requirements. *Numeracy* • a statistical analysis of data received from surveys • an analysis of retention and achievement targets compared to previous years • an analysis of skills scans results • an evaluation of initial and diagnostic assessment results. *ICT* • a visual recording of you using technology which you have adapted to meet the needs of your learners, for example, uploading materials, communicating, negotiating work activities and agreeing deadlines • audio, digital and electronic materials and records • emails • online communications, polls and surveys • online learning preference questionnaire results and how they inform the planning process. An anonymised case study demonstrating how you have applied the minimum core elements when planning inclusive teaching and learning. Your assessor's observation report and feedback, along with records of any discussions.

7 BE ABLE TO EVALUATE OWN PRACTICE WHEN PLANNING INCLUSIVE TEACHING AND LEARNING

This chapter is in two parts. The first part: **Self-assessment activities**, contains questions and activities which relate to the fourth learning outcome of the Certificate in Education and Training unit Planning to meet the needs of learners in education and training.

The assessment criteria are shown in boxes and are followed by questions and activities for you to carry out. Ensure your responses are *specific to you*, the *subject* you will teach and the *context* and *environment* in which you will teach. As this unit is at level 4, you should use academic writing and referencing when responding to the questions. When referring to a quote, make sure you understand what the quote means and how it will fit within your writing. It could be that you agree with what the author has said and it supports what you are saying, or it could be that you totally disagree with it. If so, explain why you agree or disagree and, if it's the latter, state what you would do differently. You need to write what you think, or what your point of view is, and relate it to your specialist subject.

After completing the activities, check your responses with the second part: **Guidance for evidencing achievement**. This guidance is not intended to give you the answers to questions you may be asked in any formal assessments; however, it will help you focus your responses towards meeting the assessment criteria.

At the end of the chapter is an example of a completed **Assessment grid** which gives ideas for evidence you could provide towards meeting the assessment criteria. Evidence can be cross-referenced between units and assessment criteria if it meets the requirements.

Self-assessment activities

> 4.1 Review the effectiveness of own practice when planning to meet the individual needs of learners, taking account of the views of learners and others

Q32 How can you review the effectiveness of your own practice?

Q33 Obtain feedback from your learners and others regarding the planning process to ensure you have met the individual needs of your learners.

Q34 Review the effectiveness of your practice based on the feedback you have received.

> 4.2 Identify areas for improvement in own planning to meet the individual needs of learners

Q35 Based on the feedback you have received, what areas have you identified which require improvement in relation to meeting the individual needs of learners when planning?

Guidance for evidencing achievement

> 4.1 Review the effectiveness of own practice when planning to meet the individual needs of learners, taking account of the views of learners and others

Q32 How can you review the effectiveness of your own practice?

Your response could state that the process of reviewing your own practice involves self-reflection which should be used regularly and become a part of your everyday activities. All reflection should lead to an improvement in practice; however, there may be events you would not want to change or improve as you felt they went well. If this is the case, reflect as to why they went well and use these methods in future sessions. As you become more experienced at reflective practice, you will see how you can improve and develop further. There may be aspects of your practice that will need time for changes or improvements to take effect. You might need to attend training, or devise something new before you can try out these changes.

Reviewing your progress will help you learn about yourself and what you could improve. For example, how you react to different situations or learners, how patient you are and what skills you may need to develop. You might also decide you need further training or support to improve your subject knowledge, your teaching/assessing skills and/or English, maths and ICT skills.

You could research various models of reflective practice by reading relevant text books and/or accessing the internet. You could then select one that you feel is appropriate to the context of your practice. Any model you select should be simple and straightforward so that you can relate to it.

There are many ways of recording your reflections and you should select the ones that best meet your needs. For example, you might consider how effective (or not) the initial and diagnostic assessment activities were. You could develop these reflections and note them in a journal or diary (written, visual or audio). You could then refer to a model such as Brookfield's (1995) four points of view when looking at your practice, which he called critical lenses. These lenses are from the point of view of:

- the teacher

- the learner

- colleagues

- theories and literature

Using these points of view will help you reflect upon a situation and see it in a different perspective. Skilled teachers will try to see themselves as their learners see them. Brookfield believes that *'of all the pedagogic tasks that teachers face, getting inside students' heads is one of the trickiest. It is also the most crucial'* (1995: 92).

You could read your organisation's last Ofsted inspection report (if applicable) regarding the use of initial and diagnostic assessment, and how teachers plan their sessions. You could review the strengths and areas for improvement, relate these to your own practice and identify if you need to make any changes as a result.

You should keep evidence of what you have done to show your assessor, who might also observe you with your learners. Be prepared to justify all your decisions.

Q33 Obtain feedback from your learners and others regarding the planning process to ensure you have met the individual needs of your learners.

This is a practical task enabling you to obtain feedback from your learners and others. Feedback from learners can come via written and oral questions, online polls and surveys, questionnaires, comment/feedback forms, good news stories in newsletters and the local press, social media and any other suitable method you wish to use.

Feedback from others can include verbal and written comments from:

- appraisal and review records
- awarding organisation reports
- external inspection reports
- colleagues, managers
- good news stories, i.e. organisational newsletters, local press, online stories
- internal and external quality assurance feedback
- learner comment/feedback forms
- learning support workers, teaching assistants and volunteers
- mentors, peers
- observation reports, e.g. Ofsted, qualification observers, organisation observers
- online polls
- peer observation reports
- questionnaires
- referral agencies, i.e. Job Centre Plus, National Careers Service
- regional and/or national magazine articles or reports
- self-assessment reports, i.e. those required by funding agencies
- self-evaluation forms
- surveys
- workplace supervisors

and anyone else who has an interest in planning an inclusive learning experience for your learners.

Feedback about the way in which you implement the planning process can be obtained formally via external quality assurance or inspection reports or informally via meetings with your mentor and colleagues.

You should obtain the feedback in the most appropriate way, which might include using your own methods, or those of the organisation. You could include a statistical analysis of the feedback received, including bar charts, pie charts and/or line graphs.

You should keep evidence of what you have done to show your assessor, who might also observe you with your learners. Be prepared to justify all your decisions.

Evidence could include anonymised completed copies of:

- awarding organisation reports

- external inspection reports, i.e. Ofsted

- good news stories, i.e. organisational newsletters, local press

- internal and external quality assurer feedback

- learner comment/feedback forms

- online polls

- questionnaires

- regional and/or national magazine articles, or reports which may be online

- self-assessment reports required by funding agencies

- self-evaluation forms

- surveys

Q34 Review the effectiveness of your practice based on the feedback you have received.

Based on the feedback you have received, review the effectiveness of your practice. You should consider instances of where you have received feedback for something specific.

For example:

Your ILP plans are detailed with SMART (specific, measurable, achievable, relevant and time-bound) and achievable learning goals – perhaps all learners have stated this is due to your discussing with them what their learning goals are and how they contribute towards their aspirations. They also liked the fact you discussed what they could achieve within a realistic timescale. However, you feel you could explore the range of initial and diagnostic assessments you use to find more appropriate methods of testing learners where English is a second language. This is to ensure you can engage confidently with a diverse range of learners and meet their differing needs, resulting in a positive match between the learner and your programme.

Your retention rates are higher than the target set by your organisation – the internal quality assurer has stated that your teaching and learning plans record effectively your approach to differentiation ensuring that you meet the needs of all of your learners, therefore helping to retain them. Learners state that the planned learning experience is personalised based on their interests and their preferred learning styles. To support this approach you include teaching assistants and volunteers, so that they are well briefed, and this is documented in your teaching and learning plans. They state that they are pleased with the way in which they are included in the planning process. As a result, they are better able to provide learners with the support they need to make progress. You feel your planning is thorough and takes account of individuals learning and not just your teaching. Your learners tell you during their tutorial sessions that they are enjoying learning and feel that they benefit from the extra support they receive.

You could include a summary of the feedback you have received when you evaluated the planning stages of the teaching, learning and assessment process. This could take the form of a self-evaluation section at the end of each teaching and learning session plan, or as a journal or diary (written, visual or audio) in which you note any significant incidents. You could record how you felt about the incident, what you would do differently if it happened again, and relate this to a reflective theorist.

To help you with this approach you could apply the model of reflection called Experience, Describe, Analyse, Revise (EDAR) (Gravells and Simpson, 2014). Take a situation and use the EDAR aspects to reflect upon it.

You could cross-reference your response to the unit: **Planning to meet the needs of learners in education and training** (4.2) if you have met the required criteria.

> 4.2 Identify areas for improvement in own planning to meet the individual needs of learners

Q35 What areas have you identified which require improvement in relation to meeting the individual needs of learners when planning?

This could include the fact that:

You need to access and integrate the knowledge and skills of specialist staff – some learners stated that they would have felt more confident if they had been offered a short introductory programme which included a refresher on study skills, particularly developing skills in research and writing assignments. You will speak to the appropriate staff in your organisation to plan a short programme that could be delivered by both you and a functional skills specialist.

You need to keep up to date with changes in the education sector that affect you and your learners. You have several learners who have been referred to your programme by Job Centre Plus to help them gain qualifications to enhance their job prospects. You will need to find out, within the boundaries of your role, if there are any specific responsibilities that you need to be aware of. If appropriate, you will need to liaise with Job Centre Plus staff to update them on learner punctuality and attendance. You will also need to liaise with your teaching assistants and volunteers to ensure they are informed.

You should relate your response to a reflective theory such as Schön (1983) who suggests two methods of reflection:

- reflection *in* action

- reflection *on* action

Reflection in action happens at the time of the incident, is often unconscious, is proactive and allows immediate changes to take place. For example, if you see that some learners are confused by an initial assessment question, you will rephrase it straight away.

Reflection on action takes place after the incident, is a more conscious process and is reactive. This allows you time to think about the incident, consider a different approach, or to talk to others about it before making changes. However, it might not allow you to deal with a situation as it occurs. For example, if you chose not to rephrase a question at the time, it might have had a negative impact upon the initial assessment process. However, you would be able to change it for future learners.

You could create an action plan identifying areas for your own improvement, with realistic target dates.

You could produce an anonymised case study which covers the full process of designing a survey, implementing it, analysing the results, and identifying the areas which are effective, and which need improvement, regarding the planning process. The survey should take into account the views of your learners and others.

You could cross-reference your response to the unit: Planning to meet the needs of learners in education and training (4.1) if you have met the required criteria.

Theory focus

References and further information

Brookfield, S (1995) *Becoming a Critically Reflective Teacher*. San Francisco: Jossey-Bass.

Gravells, A and Simpson, S (2014) *The Certificate in Education and Training*. London Learning Matters SAGE.

Martin, K (1996) 'Critical incidents in teaching and learning,' *Issues of Teaching and Learning*, 2 (8).

Roffey-Barentsen, J and Malthouse, R (2013) *Reflective Practice in Education and Training* (2nd edn). London: Learning Matters SAGE.

Rushton, I and Suter, M (2012) *Reflective Practice for Teaching in Lifelong Learning*. Maidenhead: OU Press.

Schön, D (1983) *The Reflective Practitioner: How Professionals Think in Action*. New York: Basic Books.

Websites

Online surveys – www.surveymonkey.com

Reflective practice – http://www.brainboxx.co.uk/a3_aspects/pages/Reflective.htm

UNIT TITLE: Planning to meet the needs of learners in education and training

Assessment grid

Learning Outcomes The learner will:	Assessment Criteria The learner can:	Example evidence
4. Be able to evaluate own practice when planning inclusive teaching and learning	4.1 Review the effectiveness of own practice when planning to meet the individual needs of learners, taking account of the views of learners and others	An explanation of how you can review the effectiveness of your own practice. A reflective learning journal or diary (written, visual or audio), which reviews the effectiveness of the planning process and relates your entries to a model of reflective practice. A written review of the effectiveness of your own practice. For example, revisiting the way learning goals are agreed with learners. A written review of the effectiveness of your own practice compared to your organisation's last Ofsted report (if applicable). Documents which relate to planning, for example, scheme of work, teaching and learning plans, initial/diagnostic assessments, individual learning plans, showing how you have reviewed their effectiveness. Anonymised completed copies of appraisal and review records, awarding organisation reports, internal quality assurer feedback, learner comment/feedback forms, Ofsted reports, online polls, questionnaires and surveys. Specific comments and feedback received from others, whether positive or negative. A statistical analysis of the feedback received, including bar charts, pie charts and/or line graphs. Cross-referenced to the unit: Planning to meet the needs of learners in education and training (4.2).
	4.2 Identify areas for improvement in own planning to meet the individual needs of learners	A written identification of areas which require improvement, relating them to your own planning practice. For example, using more specialist staff during the initial assessment process. An action plan identifying areas for your own improvement, with realistic target dates. An anonymised case study which covers the full process of designing a survey, implementing it, analysing the results, and identifying the areas which are effective, and which need improvement. The case study should relate to the planning process and take into account the views of learners and others. Cross-referenced to the unit: Planning to meet the needs of learners in education and training (4.1).

8 BE ABLE TO USE INCLUSIVE TEACHING AND LEARNING APPROACHES IN ACCORDANCE WITH INTERNAL AND EXTERNAL REQUIREMENTS

This chapter is in two parts. The first part: **Self-assessment activities**, contains questions and activities which relate to the first learning outcome of the Certificate in Education and Training unit Delivering education and training.

The assessment criteria are shown in boxes and are followed by questions and activities for you to carry out. Ensure your responses are *specific to you*, the *subject* you will teach and the *context* and *environment* in which you will teach. When using a quote, make sure you understand what the quote means and how it will fit within your writing. It could be that you agree with what the author has said and it supports what you are saying, or it could be that you totally disagree with it. If so, explain why you agree or disagree and, if it's the latter, state what you would do differently. You need to write what you think, or what your point of view is, and relate it to your specialist subject.

After completing the activities, check your responses with the second part: **Guidance for evidencing achievement**. This guidance is not intended to give you the answers to questions you may be asked in any formal assessments; however, it will help you focus your responses towards meeting the assessment criteria.

At the end of the chapter is an example of a completed **Assessment grid** which gives ideas for evidence you could provide towards meeting the assessment criteria. Evidence can be cross-referenced between units and assessment criteria if it meets the requirements.

Self-assessment activities

> 1.1 Analyse the effectiveness of teaching and learning approaches used in own area of specialism in relation to meeting the individual needs of learners

Q36 What teaching and learning approaches can you use for your subject specialism?

Q37 Analyse the effectiveness of these approaches in relation to meeting the individual needs of your learners.

1.2 Create an inclusive teaching and learning environment

Q38 Demonstrate how you create an inclusive teaching and learning environment with your learners.

1.3 Demonstrate an inclusive approach to teaching and learning in accordance with internal and external requirements

Q39 During your sessions, demonstrate an inclusive approach to teaching and learning in accordance with internal and external requirements. Internal requirements might include embedding English, maths and information and communication technology (ICT). External requirements will include those imposed by awarding and regulatory organisations.

Guidance for evidencing achievement

> 1.1 Analyse the effectiveness of teaching and learning approaches used in own area of specialism in relation to meeting the individual needs of learners

Q36 What teaching and learning approaches can you use for your subject specialism?

Your response should list the teaching and learning approaches which are relevant for your specialist subject. For example:

- discussion

- finishing activity

- online research

- paired activity

- practical task

- questions

- quiz

- role play

- starter activity

- visiting speakers

The activities you choose should be realistic and achievable for your learners and you should be confident that they can be delivered and completed within the time allocated. Your list should include approaches that you could use at the beginning, in the middle and at the end of your session. For example:

- the *beginning* – a starter activity such as an icebreaker is a good way of everyone getting to know each other's name, and encouraging communication to take place. It will also help you to begin to assess the dynamics of the group

- the *middle* – a variety of approaches such as discussion, paired activity, practical work, online research, role play and visiting speakers

- the *end* – a finishing activity based on the topic of your session such as asking individual questions or holding a group quiz to check knowledge

Differentiating your teaching, learning and assessment approaches should lead to more confident learners who feel included, are motivated to learn and are able to achieve. Whilst it may take longer to plan and prepare your sessions to differentiate effectively, you will find your learners are more engaged and motivated rather than being bored and uninterested.

Q37 Analyse the effectiveness of these approaches in relation to meeting the individual needs of your learners.

Your response will depend upon the subject and level you are teaching, the context and environment you are teaching in, the length of each session and any particular learner needs. It's not about what you will teach, but how your learners will learn.

You could analyse how each of your approaches you listed in your response to Q36 will include your learners in relevant activities during the session, rather than exclude anyone for any reason. The best way to ensure you are effectively including all learners and treating them equally is to ask them if there is anything you can do to help, or that can be done differently for them. To value and promote equality and diversity among your learners, you need to embrace their differences, and encourage interaction and support, challenging any negative actions or beliefs.

Approaches should always be fit for purpose, i.e. to enable learning to take place, and not just used for the sake of it, or because you like to do things in a certain way. It is very rare that you will have a group of learners who are all at the same level of ability, with the same prior knowledge and experience, and with the same needs. The approaches you use need to be adaptable to ensure that you can take individual needs into account.

To meet the individual needs of your learners you will need to differentiate your approaches. Differentiation is about using a range of different activities and resources to meet the needs of individuals and groups. You use should recognise that each of your learners is different from other learners in many ways, and therefore should not be excluded from any activities for any legitimate reason.

You could differentiate activities by the learners' learning preference, level of ability, level of qualification, past experiences or current knowledge. Small-group work and paired activities are a good way to use differentiation. For example, a learner who is an activist may benefit from being grouped with a learner who is a reflector. The learners might then adopt some of the alternative preferences.

Your response could include Petty's (2009: 587-588) summary of key differentiation strategies as 'differentiation by:

- task

- outcome

- time allowed

- accommodating different learning styles and support needs

- setting individual tasks and targets'

You could produce an anoymised case study regarding the approaches and activities you have used with your learners and how they met individual needs.

Evidence could include activities you have used with learners such as a practical task, along with an analysis of how it met individual learner needs.

You could cross-reference your response to the unit Delivering education and training (1.3) if you have met the required criteria.

1.2 Create an inclusive teaching and learning environment

Q38 Demonstrate how you create an inclusive teaching and learning environment with your learners.

This is a practical task enabling you to demonstrate how you create an inclusive teaching and learning environment with your learners. Inclusive learning should ensure a match between each individual's requirements and the provision that is made for them. If you ever feel unsure as to whether you, or other learners and colleagues are valuing equality and diversity, just ask yourself: is this fair? Or, how would I feel in this situation? Or, would I want to be treated in this way? If your answer is a negative one, then make sure you do something about it. It is your responsibility to ensure that you provide an inclusive learning environment and equality of opportunity regarding all aspects of the learning experience.

You could plan different activities which all your learners are capable of achieving, as well as what most or some can achieve according to their level and ability. This should be reflected in your teaching and learning plan. However, this can change as the session continues depending upon the progress being made.

To help create an inclusive teaching and learning environment, you should:

- create, design and/or select appropriate resources and activities

- organise specialist help when needed

- encourage social, cultural and recreational activities relevant to the programme (if possible)

- provide opportunities for comments, feedback and suggestions

- give honest information about the programme and how it will be organised, delivered and assessed

- signpost and offer guidance towards other learning opportunities and/or access to additional support

You should keep evidence of what you have done to show your assessor, who might also observe you with your learners. Be prepared to justify all your decisions.

Evidence could include anonymised initial assessment records, teaching and learning plans, learning agreements/contracts, individual learning plans (ILPs)/action plans, and your organisation's learner entitlement statement (if applicable). Evidence should also show what adjustments you have made to enable the creation of an inclusive teaching and learning environment with your learners.

1.3 Demonstrate an inclusive approach to teaching and learning in accordance with internal and external requirements

Q39 During your sessions, demonstrate an inclusive approach to teaching and learning in accordance with internal and external requirements. Internal requirements might include embedding English, maths and information and communication technology (ICT). External requirements will include those imposed by awarding and regulatory organisations.

This is a practical task enabling you to demonstrate an inclusive approach with your learners. You could produce a written or video case study in accordance with internal and external requirements. This would require permission and the co-operation of your learners and anyone else involved. This type of evidence could be highly valued by Ofsted (if applicable), the regulatory body for inspecting teaching, learning and assessment. Hearing and seeing the impact of your approach to meeting your learner's individual needs can be very honest and powerful.

The recording should be able to demonstrate the inclusive approaches you have used. It should also show that internal (organisation) requirements are met, for example, embedding English, maths and ICT, and external (awarding organisation) are also met, for example the timing of assessments.

Evidence could include anonymised initial assessment records, teaching and learning plans and individual learning plans (ILPs)/action plans. Evidence should also show what adjustments you have made to enable the creation of an inclusive teaching and learning environment with your learners.

Theory focus

References and further information

Fawbert, F (2008) *Teaching in Post-Compulsory Education*. London: Continuum Publishing Ltd.

Gould, J (2012) *Learning Theory and Classroom Practice in the Lifelong Learning Sector*. London: SAGE Publications.

Gravells, A and Simpson, S (2014) *The Certificate in Education and Training*. London: Learning Matters SAGE.

Ingle, S and Duckworth, V (2013) *Teaching and Training Vocational Learners*. London: Learning Matters SAGE.

Kidd, W and Czerniawski, G (2010) *Successful Teaching 14–19*. London: SAGE Publications.

Peart, S and Atkins, L (2011) *Teaching 14–19 Learners in the Lifelong Learning Sector*. London: Learning Matters SAGE.

Petty, G (2009) *Teaching Today: A Practical Guide*. Cheltenham: Nelson Thornes.

Rogers, A and Horrocks, N (2010) *Teaching Adults* (4th edn). Maidenhead: OU Press.

Websites

Differentiation – http://geoffpetty.com/wp-content/uploads/2012/12/0DIFFERENTIATIONwhatand how2.doc

Ofsted – ofsted.gov.uk

Teaching and learning theories – http://classweb.gmu.edu/ndabbagh/Resources/IDKB/models_ theories.htm

Teacher training videos for using ICT – www.teachertrainingvideos.com/latest.html

Theories of learning – www.learningandteaching.info/learning/

Tips for teaching adults – http://www.helium.com/knowledge/61278-tips-for-teaching-adult-learners-instead-of-younger-learners

UNIT TITLE: Delivering education and training

Assessment grid

Learning Outcomes The learner will:	Assessment Criteria The learner can:	Example evidence
1. Be able to use inclusive teaching and learning approaches in accordance with internal and external requirements	1.1 Analyse the effectiveness of teaching and learning approaches used in own area of specialism in relation to meeting the individual needs of learners	A list of teaching and learning approaches you could use for your subject, such as discussion, paired activity, questions, quiz and role play. An analysis of the approaches you have listed, stating how you could use them for your specialist subject and how they meet individual needs. Evidence of activities you have used with learners such as a practical task, along with an analysis of how it met individual learner needs. An anonymised case study analysing the effectiveness of the teaching and learning approaches you have used to meet the individual needs of your learners. Your assessor's observation report and feedback, along with records of any discussions. Cross-referenced to the unit Delivering education and training (1.3).
	1.2 Create an inclusive teaching and learning environment	Anonymised initial assessment records, teaching and learning plans, learning agreements/contracts, individual learning plans (ILPs)/action plans, and your organisation's learner entitlement statement (if applicable). Evidence of adjustments you have made to enable the creation of an inclusive teaching and learning environment, for example, amended ground rules, activities which have been adapted and resources which have been changed. Your assessor's observation report and feedback, along with records of any discussions.
	1.3 Demonstrate an inclusive approach to teaching and learning in accordance with internal and external requirements	A written or video case study which demonstrates an inclusive approach to teaching and learning in accordance with internal and external requirements (with the required permissions). Anonymised initial assessment records, teaching and learning plans and individual learning plans (ILPs)/action plans. Your assessor's observation report and feedback, along with records of any discussions.

9 BE ABLE TO COMMUNICATE WITH LEARNERS AND OTHER LEARNING PROFESSIONALS TO PROMOTE LEARNING AND PROGRESSION

This chapter is in two parts. The first part: **Self-assessment activities**, contains questions and activities which relate to the second learning outcome of the Certificate in Education and Training unit Delivering education and training.

The assessment criteria are shown in boxes and are followed by questions and activities for you to carry out. Ensure your responses are *specific to you*, the *subject* you will teach and the *context* and *environment* in which you will teach. When using a quote, make sure you understand what the quote means and how it will fit within your writing. It could be that you agree with what the author has said and it supports what you are saying, or it could be that you totally disagree with it. If so, explain why you agree or disagree and, if it's the latter, state what you would do differently. You need to write what you think, or what your point of view is, and relate it to your specialist subject.

After completing the activities, check your responses with the second part: **Guidance for evidencing achievement**. This guidance is not intended to give you the answers to questions you may be asked in any formal assessments; however, it will help you focus your responses towards meeting the assessment criteria.

At the end of the chapter is an example of a completed **Assessment grid** which gives ideas for evidence you could provide towards meeting the assessment criteria. Evidence can be cross-referenced between units and assessment criteria if it meets the requirements.

Self-assessment activities

> 2.1 Analyse benefits and limitations of communication methods and media used in own area of specialism

Q40 What communication methods and media can you use with learners for your specialist subject?

Q41 Analyse the benefits and limitations of the communication methods you identified in your response to Q40.

2.2 Use communication methods and media to meet individual learner needs

Q42 During your sessions, demonstrate the use of communication methods and media to meet the individual needs of your learners.

2.3 Communicate with other learning professionals to meet individual learner needs and encourage progression

Q43 With whom could you communicate regarding meeting the individual needs of your learners and encouraging their progression?

Q44 Communicate with the learning professionals you have identified in your response to Q43 and keep anonymised records.

Guidance for evidencing achievement

2.1 Analyse benefits and limitations of communication methods and media used in own area of specialism

Q40 What communication methods and media can you use with learners for your specialist subject?

Your response should state that communication methods can be verbal, non-verbal or written. The methods you use to communicate with your learners will depend on their individual needs and what you want to convey. Your knowledge of your specialist subject will help you decide with confidence how you are going to do this. Whichever method you use you should try to keep things simple, and ensure that what you are communicating is accurate, not ambiguous or biased, and is expressed in a professional manner.

Your response could include the following communication methods and media:

Verbal

- face to face, for example, discussions and questions

- live online voice and video calls, for example, a one-to-one tutorial or a conference with colleagues

- telephone, for example, exchanging information

Non-verbal

- body language, for example, not folding arms

- eye contact and smiling, for example, giving reassurance

- listening, for example, conscious listening with a purpose and nodding to affirm understanding

Written

- emails and correspondence

- feedback and tutorial records

- handouts

- interactive whiteboard

- online forums

- mobile text messaging

- presentations

- virtual learning environment (VLE)

Understanding a little about your own personal communication style will help you create a lasting impression upon your learners and enable you to become a better listener. If you are aware of how others see and hear you, you can adapt to suit their style of communication.

You should relate your response to a quote such as 'Good communicators succeed in choosing the best medium of communication for the particular purpose in mind' (The Times 100 Business Case Studies, date accessed 18 November 2013).

You could cross-reference your response to the unit **Delivering education and training** (2.2 and 2.3) if you have met the required criteria.

Q41 Analyse the benefits and limitations of the communication methods you identified in your response to Q40

You could produce a table and complete it with the benefits and limitations of the methods and media you identified in relation to your specialist subject:

Method	Type/media	Benefit	Limitation
Verbal	Telephone, face-to-face discussion, online audio and video calls	Instant ability to question and clarify	No record of the conversation unless it is recorded
Non-verbal	Eye contact and smiling	Provides reassurance	May be misunderstood
Written	Text message, email, correspondence	Provides a record of the communication	Not always accessible

Your response should then analyse the communication methods in more detail. For example:

Verbal

- Benefit – face-to-face discussion can help you gauge a learner's response by reading their body language and actively participating in dialogue

- Limitation – difficult to refute any points of discussion as there is nothing in writing supporting the messages communicated. It is not suitable for future reference unless it has been recorded

Non-verbal

- Benefit – eye contact and smiling can convey a positive message to the person with whom you are communicating

- Limitation – being able to hide how you feel, i.e. controlling your non-verbal signals

Written

- Benefit – emails and correspondence can be most appropriate when detailed instructions are required, and when something needs to be documented

- Limitation – some forms of written communication can take longer to get to your learner, i.e. if they are mailed, or not accessible online

You should relate your response to a quote such as '*Our bodies give away far more information than we realise. In fact, you could say that bodies don't talk: they shout. Body language includes facial expression, gestures and posture. It's difficult to decide which of these three is the most important in teaching, but facial expression must be a strong contender*' (Appleyard and Appleyard, 2010: 33).

2.2 Use communication methods and media to meet individual learner needs

---

Q42 During your sessions, demonstrate the use of communication methods and media to meet the individual needs of your learners.

This is a practical task enabling you to demonstrate the use of communication methods and media to meet the individual needs of your learners. You should keep evidence of what you have done to show your assessor, who might also observe you with your learners. Be prepared to justify all your decisions.

You could make a visual recording of your session which shows the different communication methods and media you used. Just make sure you obtain the relevant permissions.

2.3 Communicate with other learning professionals to meet individual learner needs and encourage progression

---

Q43 With whom could you communicate regarding meeting the individual needs of your learners and encouraging their progression?

Your response should list the other learning professionals that you communicate with regarding meeting the individual needs of your learners, and encouraging their progression. These could include:

- colleagues

- external inspectors

- internal quality assurers

- specialist learning support staff

- staff from referral agencies

- teaching assistants

Your response could state how you would improve the way you communicate to help your learners progress further. For example, reading current literature to find out ways in which to communicate with a learner who has a particular need such as diabetes. Whom you communicate with and how you do it should have the aim of encouraging your learners to progress towards achieving their chosen goal.

Q44 Communicate with the learning professionals you have identified in your response to Q43 and keep anonymised records.

This is a practical task enabling you to communicate with learning professionals and keep anonymised records. You should keep evidence of what you have done to show your assessor, who might also observe you with your learners. Be prepared to justify all your decisions.

It is important that you have an organised and formal approach to communications with others when the discussions involve your learners. If you are going to have regular contact with some professionals regarding your learners you should agree what the protocols are. You should always record the details of the communication, i.e. who, what, when, where, why and how. There should also be a record of any actions agreed and who is responsible for carrying them out. You could create a contacts sheet for this purpose if your organisation doesn't already have one. This would list all those people you will communicate with, along with their contact details such as telephone number and email address.

You could produce an anonymised case study regarding communicating with other learning professionals to meet the individual needs of learners. The study should show how this has impacted upon learner progression.

Evidence could include organisational policies and procedures regarding communicating with other learning professionals, along with records of communication such as emails and contact logs.

Theory focus

References and further information

Appleyard, N and Appleyard, K (2010) *Communicating with Learners in the Lifelong Learning Sector*. London: Learning Matters SAGE.

Gould, J (2012) *Learning Theory and Classroom Practice in the Lifelong Learning Sector*. London: SAGE Publications.

Gravells, A and Simpson, S (2014) *The Certificate in Education and Training*. London: Learning Matters SAGE.

Ingle, S and Duckworth, V (2013) *Enhancing Learning through Technology in Lifelong Learning – Fresh Ideas: Innovative Strategies*. Oxford: OU Press.

Mehrabian, A (1981) *Silent Messages: Implicit Communication of Emotions and Attitudes*. Belmont, CA: Wadsworth.

Rogers, A and Horrocks, N (2010) *Teaching Adults* (4th edn). Maidenhead: OU Press.

Younie, S and Leask, M (2013) *Teaching with Technologies: The Essential Guide*. Maidenhead: McGraw Hill.

Websites

The Times 100 Business Case Studies – http://businesscasestudies.co.uk/hmrc/getting-the-message-across-the-importance-of-good-communications/methods-of-communication.

Using computers and technology: free guides – http://digitalunite.com/

Using IT – www.reading.ac.uk/internal/its/training/its-training-index.aspx

Using VLEs – www.ofsted.gov.uk/resources/virtual-learning-environments-e-portfolio

Video email – http://mailvu.com/

UNIT TITLE: Delivering education and training
Assessment grid

Learning Outcomes The learner will:	Assessment Criteria The learner can:	Example evidence
2. Be able to communicate with learners and other learning professionals to promote learning and progression	2.1 Analyse benefits and limitations of communication methods and media used in own area of specialism	An analysis of the benefits and limitations of verbal, non-verbal and written communication methods and media. A table detailing relevant examples of verbal, non-verbal and written communication and media used for your specialist subject. Evidence of the communication methods and media you have used with your learners for your specialist subject such as discussions, letters, emails. Cross-referenced to the unit Delivering education and training (2.2 and 2.3).
	2.2 Use communication methods and media to meet individual learner needs	Evidence of teaching and learning plans showing the communication methods used. Evidence of adjustments made to the communication methods and media used to meet the individual needs of your learners. A visual recording of your session which shows the different communication methods and media you used (with relevant permissions). Your assessor's observation report and feedback, along with records of any discussions.
	2.3 Communicate with other learning professionals to meet individual learner needs and encourage progression	A list of other learning professionals with whom you communicate. Anonymised records showing contact with others such as emails. Evidence of organisational policies and procedures regarding communication with others. An anonymised case study regarding communicating with other learning professionals to meet the individual needs of learners. The study should show how this has impacted upon learner progression. Your assessor's observation report and feedback, along with records of any discussions.

10 BE ABLE TO USE TECHNOLOGIES IN DELIVERING INCLUSIVE TEACHING AND LEARNING

This chapter is in two parts. The first part: **Self-assessment activities**, contains questions and activities which relate to the third learning outcome of the Certificate in Education and Training unit Delivering education and training.

The assessment criteria are shown in boxes and are followed by questions and activities for you to carry out. Ensure your responses are *specific to you*, the *subject* you will teach and the *context* and *environment* in which you will teach. When using a quote, make sure you understand what the quote means and how it will fit within your writing. It could be that you agree with what the author has said and it supports what you are saying, or it could be that you totally disagree with it. If so, explain why you agree or disagree and, if it's the latter, state what you would do differently. You need to write what you think, or what your point of view is, and relate it to your specialist subject.

After completing the activities, check your responses with the second part: **Guidance for evidencing achievement**. This guidance is not intended to give you the answers to questions you may be asked in any formal assessments; however, it will help you focus your responses towards meeting the assessment criteria.

At the end of the chapter is an example of a completed **Assessment grid** which gives ideas for evidence you could provide towards meeting the assessment criteria. Evidence can be cross-referenced between units and assessment criteria if it meets the requirements.

Self-assessment activities

3.1 Analyse benefits and limitations of technologies used in own area of specialism

Q45 What technologies can you use for your specialist subject?

Q46 Analyse the benefits and limitations of those technologies you listed in your response to Q45.

3.2 Use technologies to enhance teaching and meet individual learner needs

Q47 During your sessions, demonstrate the use of technology to enhance teaching and to meet individual learner needs.

Guidance for evidencing achievement

3.1 Analyse benefits and limitations of technologies used in own area of specialism

Q45 What technologies can you use for your specialist subject?

Your response should list the types and methods of technology you can use which are appropriate to your specialist subject. Information and communication technology (ICT) covers a wide range, and your list might include some of the following:

- applications (apps) and relevant computer programs
- audio, video, digital and online clips (creating or viewing, recorded or live)
- blogs
- calculators
- chat rooms
- cloud-based applications
- computer programs
- digital cameras, camcorders and video recorders
- discussion boards
- distance/online/open learning
- e-assessments
- electronic brain games
- email (text and video, with or without attachments)
- e-portfolios and e-assessment
- e-readers
- file-sharing websites
- graphic organisers
- interactive and online programs and educational games
- interactive whiteboards linked to the internet
- internet/intranet access
- laptops, netbooks and tablets
- mobile phones and smart phones
- online discussions
- online voting
- podcasts
- presentation packages
- robotics
- scanners
- social networking (if appropriate)
- smart boards
- three-dimensional printers
- video conferencing and video email
- virtual learning environments (VLEs)
- webcasts, weblogs, short messages
- webinars
- websites which are interactive for creating and using surveys, polls and questionnaires
- wikis

Q46 Analyse the benefits and limitations of those technologies you listed in your response to Q45.

You could design a table listing the technologies you use and analysing the benefits and limitations of each.

For example:

Technology	Benefits	Limitations
Distance learning: learning which takes place away from the organisation offering the programme/ qualification	Work can be posted (online or manually) to learners and returned for assessment Learning can occur at a time and place to suit the learner Can be combined with other learning methods, for example, workshop activities	Could be a long gap between submitting work for assessment and receiving feedback Self-discipline is needed Targets must be clearly agreed Learner may never meet teacher/assessor
Interactive whiteboard: teachers and learners can use various functions including linking to the internet	Useful for group work and presentations	Not all learners can use it at the same time Some learners might not be confident at using it
Podcast: a digital, audio or video file of the session which is uploaded to the internet	Useful if learners cannot attend a session, or wish to hear it again, as they can listen or watch it at a time to suit	Some learners might not be able to access them May encourage non-attendance

The benefits you identify should reinforce that it is the purposeful use of information learning technology (ILT) which provides your learners with a reason to use and engage with it. Limitations or infrequent use of technology will not encourage your learners to use it as an integral part of their learning. For example, you might only use video clips to enhance their learning experience when you know you are being observed by your assessor.

Your response should state that whichever types of technology you decide to use, you must ensure that it is being used for a meaningful purpose. For example, uploading materials and resources for learners to access in their own time to support the current topic.

You should relate your response to a quote such as: 'Advances in new technologies are making it easier to meet the needs of individual learners. Not only can learning environments be structured so that the learners can set the pace of their learning and control the delivery of information, but, increasingly, e-learning is able to cater for the individual learning styles of the students' (Holmes and Gardner, 2006: 66).

You could produce an anonymised case study regarding a real activity that ensures your learners understand why they are using the technology and what benefits they are getting from it.

You could also make a visual, aural or digital recording of you using technology with learners. Just make sure you obtain the relevant permissions.

You could cross-reference your response to the unit Delivering education and training (3.2) if you have met the required criteria.

> 3.2 Use technologies to enhance teaching and meet individual learner needs

Q47 During your sessions, demonstrate the use of technology to enhance teaching and to meet individual learner needs.

This is a practical task enabling you to demonstrate the use of technology to enhance teaching and to meet individual learner needs. You should keep evidence of what you have done to show your assessor, who might also observe you with your learners. Be prepared to justify all your decisions.

Technology can help overcome barriers to learning; for example, pairing an experienced learner with an inexperienced learner so that someone who hasn't used it before doesn't feel alone. You need to be careful that learners are using it appropriately, i.e. not accessing unsuitable websites or using social network sites while you think they are working. Some learners may be concerned about using technology; for example, a learner with epilepsy may need regular breaks from a computer screen. You could let your learners bring laptops, tablets and e-readers to use for reading downloaded texts and/or writing notes rather than using hard-copy textbooks, pen and paper. You will need to be careful that some learners do not feel excluded because they are not able to afford this type of technology and may therefore feel isolated.

You could ask your observer to focus your next observation on how effectively your learners are using technology to support their learning. Prior to the observation, you could research Ofsted's criteria relating to learners' use of technology. Find out what their expectations are and ask for feedback from your observer as to how well you met the requirements.

Evidence should include examples of technology you have used, for example, distance-learning materials, interactive whiteboard presentations and podcasts.

Theory focus

References and further information

Gravells, A and Simpson, S (2014) *The Certificate in Education and Training*. London: Learning Matters SAGE.

Haythornthwaite, C and Andrews, R (2011) *e-learning Theory and Practice*. London: Learning Matters SAGE.

Hill, C (2008) *Teaching with E-learning in the Further Education and Skills Sector* (2nd edn). Exeter: Learning Matters SAGE.

Holmes, B and Gardner, J (2006) *e-learning Concepts and Practice*. London: SAGE Publications.

Ingle, S and Duckworth, V (2013) *Enhancing Learning through Technology in Lifelong Learning – Fresh Ideas: Innovative Strategies*. Oxford: OU Press.

Websites

Classroom management free resources – http://www.pivotaleducation.com/free-resources/

Cloud computing storage – https://www.dropbox.com/

Further Education Guide to using learning technology – http://feweek.co.uk/2013/02/22/guide-to-fe-learning-tech/?goback=.gde_4139923_member_217969739

ICT free support – www.onlinebasics.co.uk and http://learn.go-on.co.uk

Ofsted – ofsted.gov.uk

Online presentations – www.prezi.com

Puzzle software – www.crossword-compiler.com; www.educational-software-directory.net/game/puzzle; http://hotpot.uvic.ca; www.mathsnet.net

Teacher training videos for using ICT – www.teachertrainingvideos.com/latest.html

Using computers and technology: free guides – http://digitalunite.com/

Using IT – www.reading.ac.uk/internal/its/training/its-training-index.aspx

Using VLEs – www.ofsted.gov.uk/resources/virtual-learning-environments-e-portfolio

Video e-mail – http://mailvu.com/

UNIT TITLE: Delivering education and training
Assessment grid

Learning Outcomes The learner will:	Assessment Criteria The learner can:	Example evidence
3. Be able to use technologies in delivering inclusive teaching and learning	3.1 Analyse benefits and limitations of technologies used in own area of specialism	A list of the types and methods of technology you use which are appropriate to your specialist subject.
		Evidence of the technology used, for example, distance learning, interactive whiteboard and podcasts.
		A table analysing the benefits and limitations of the types and methods of technology which are appropriate to your specialist subject.
		An anonymised case study regarding a real activity that ensures your learners understand why they are using the technology and what benefits they are getting from it.
		A visual, aural or digital recording of you using technology with learners (with relevant permissions).
		Your assessor's observation report and feedback, along with records of any discussions.
		Cross-referenced to the unit Delivering education and training (3.2).
	3.2 Use technologies to enhance teaching and meet individual learner needs	Evidence of technology used, for example, distance-learning materials, interactive whiteboard presentation and podcasts.
		Evidence of researching Ofsted's criteria relating to learners' use of technology and how you have met the requirements.
		Your assessor's observation report and feedback, along with records of any discussions.

11 BE ABLE TO IMPLEMENT THE MINIMUM CORE WHEN DELIVERING INCLUSIVE TEACHING AND LEARNING

This chapter is in two parts. The first part: **Self-assessment activities**, contains questions and activities which relate to the fourth learning outcome of the Certificate in Education and Training unit Delivering education and training.

The assessment criteria are shown in boxes and are followed by questions and activities for you to carry out. Ensure your responses are *specific to you*, the *subject* you will teach and the *context* and *environment* in which you will teach. When using a quote, make sure you understand what the quote means and how it will fit within your writing. It could be that you agree with what the author has said and it supports what you are saying, or it could be that you totally disagree with it. If so, explain why you agree or disagree and, if it's the latter, state what you would do differently. You need to write what you think, or what your point of view is, and relate it to your specialist subject.

After completing the activities, check your responses with the second part: **Guidance for evidencing achievement**. This guidance is not intended to give you the answers to questions you may be asked in any formal assessments; however, it will help you focus your responses towards meeting the assessment criteria.

At the end of the chapter is an example of a completed **Assessment grid** which gives ideas for evidence you could provide towards meeting the assessment criteria. Evidence can be cross-referenced between units and assessment criteria if it meets the requirements.

Self-assessment activities

> 4.1 Analyse ways in which minimum core elements can be demonstrated when delivering inclusive teaching and learning

Q48 Analyse how you can demonstrate minimum core elements when delivering inclusive teaching and learning.

> 4.2 Apply minimum core elements in delivering inclusive teaching and learning

Q49 Demonstrate how you can apply the relevant minimum core elements when delivering inclusive teaching and learning.

Guidance for evidencing achievement

> 4.1 Analyse ways in which minimum core elements can be demonstrated when delivering inclusive teaching and learning

Q48 Analyse how you can demonstrate minimum core elements when delivering inclusive teaching and learning.

Your response should analyse how you can demonstrate the different minimum core elements, i.e. literacy, language, numeracy and information and communication technology (ICT), when delivering inclusive learning. For example:

Literacy

Devising schemes of work and teaching and learning plans (session plans), annotating aspects of the qualification guidance and supporting materials regarding the delivery of your specialist subject. Creating handouts and learning materials which are clear and unambiguous. Checking spelling, grammar, punctuation and sentence construction of all documents created before issuing them to learners or uploading them to a virtual learning environment (VLE) or other system.

You should relate your response to a quote such as: *'It is always useful to have some basic strategies for supporting learners, which may include being able to offer some basic strategies for developing accuracy, for example, Look, Say, Cover, Check, (spelling); spell check, use of dictionaries'* (Skills for Business, 2007: 45).

Language

Communicating clearly and effectively with learners during sessions. Giving clear instructions to your learners when explaining activities they will be involved in. If your learners are not clear about what they are being asked to do and why, this will impact on their learning. Avoiding the use of jargon wherever possible and explaining acronyms and abbreviations. Asking questions to check a learner's knowledge and understanding, and listening to their responses. Listening to questions and answering them appropriately.

You should relate your response to a quote such as: *'There are three key areas where we need teachers to be very well equipped: subject knowledge and academic preparation, overall literacy and numeracy, and the personal and interpersonal skills that are necessary in order to interact successfully in the classroom'* (Department for Education, 2010: 20).

Numeracy

Calculating how long various activities will take which may be fairly complicated if you are delivering a range of differentiated activities for learners at different levels. Managing how long learners are actually taking to carry out an activity, and what time they have left to complete it. Evaluating how this is impacting on the timing for the rest of the session, for example, if an activity is taking longer, do you need to make alterations to the remaining time and if so, by how much?

Asking your learners to complete a list of tasks within a set time limit. This provides them with the experience of knowing the time, delegating time to certain tasks and managing their time to complete the list of tasks.

You should relate your response to a quote such as: 'Programmes for the lowest attaining learners – including many with LDD [learning difficulties and disabilities] as well as those highly disaffected with formal education – should concentrate on the core academic skills of English and maths, and on work experience' (Wolf, 2011: 16).

ICT

Creating and adapting teaching and learning materials using various applications and technology. Preparing online materials and uploading them to a VLE or other system. Using email or social networking to communicate appropriately with others. Using new technology for activities, for example, using voting pods to complete a gapped handout or using digital media for visual/audio recording and playback of activities and presentations.

Using the internet with your learners to support the completion of activities, for example, giving your learners an activity to create a presentation to deliver the results of an activity to the rest of the group.

You should relate your response to a quote such as: 'to benefit from e-learning an individual needs to have a reasonable degree of ICT [information and communication technology] skills and confidence in using technology. Tutors seeking to use e-learning methods need both technical and pedagogical skills' (Clarke and Luger, www.niace.org.uk/lifelonglearningenquiry, date accessed 19 November 2013).

4.2 Apply minimum core elements in delivering inclusive teaching and learning

---

Q49 Demonstrate how you can apply the relevant minimum core elements when delivering inclusive teaching and learning.

This is a practical task enabling you to use the minimum core elements you have analysed in Q48.

You should keep evidence of what you have done to show your assessor, who might also observe you with your learners. Be prepared to justify all your decisions.

Evidence could include:

Literacy

- action plans
- group profile
- handouts
- learning materials, for example, word activities
- programme rationale
- scheme of work
- teaching and learning plans (session plans)
- tutorial review records
- website or VLE content

Language

- a visual or digital recording of you speaking to your learners and responding to their questions (with their permission)

- a visual or digital recording of a session where you have received feedback from your learners regarding how effectively you communicated with them regarding various activities.

Numeracy

- an analysis of the timings of activities carried out by learners during sessions

- a statistical analysis of data received from surveys

- budgeting for the cost of materials, equipment and resources required throughout the programme

- scheduling and timetabling your sessions and the teaching, learning and assessment activities within them.

ICT

- a visual recording of you using technology which you have created/adapted to meet the needs of your learners for activities such as uploading materials to a VLE, communicating and negotiating work activities and agreeing deadlines with learners

- appropriate use of social networking, for example, using Twitter to send information to your learners

- audio, digital and electronic materials and records you have created and used

- emails

- online communications, polls and surveys.

You could produce a case study of how you have applied the minimum core elements; however, make sure you don't use any real names.

Theory focus

References and further information

Appleyard, N and Appleyard, K (2009) *The Minimum Core for Language and Literacy*. London: Learning Matters SAGE.

Clark, A (2009) *The Minimum Core for Information and Communication Technology*. London: Learning Matters SAGE.

Coffield, F (2008) *Just Suppose Teaching and Learning Became the First Priority*. London: Learning and Skills Network.

Department for Education (2010) *The Importance of Teaching Schools* (White Paper). London: Department for Education.

Friedman, M (2009) *Trying Hard Is Not Good Enough*. Santa Fe, NM: FPSI Publishing (Kindle version).

Gravells, A and Simpson, S (2014) *The Certificate in Education and Training*. London: Learning Matters SAGE.

LLUK (2007) *Literacy, Language, Numeracy and ICT: Inclusive Learning Approaches for all Teachers, Tutors and Trainers in the Learning and Skills Sector*. London: Lifelong Learning UK.

LSIS (2007, revised 2013) *Addressing Literacy, Language, Numeracy and ICT Needs in Education and Training: Defining the Minimum Core of Teachers' Knowledge, Understanding and Personal Skills – A Guide for Initial Teacher Education Programmes*. Coventry: LSIS.

Peart, S (2009) *The Minimum Core for Numeracy*. London: Learning Matters SAGE.

Skills for Business (2007) *Inclusive Learning Approaches for Literacy, Language, Numeracy and ICT: Companion Guide to the Minimum Core*. Nottingham: DfES Publications.

Wolf, A (2011) *Wolf Review of Vocational Education Government Response*. London: Department for Education.

Websites

Assessment tools (literacy, numeracy, ESOL, dyslexia) – www.excellencegateway.org.uk/toolslibrary

Approved literacy and numeracy qualifications – http://www.ifl.ac.uk/__data/assets/pdf_file/0006/27753/Level-2-Literacy-and-Numeracy-Skills-_June-2012.pdf

Computer free support – www.onlinebasics.co.uk and http://learn.go-on.co.uk

Digital Unite – http://digitalunite.com/guides

Digital technologies for education and research – www.jisc.ac.uk

English and maths free support – www.move-on.org.uk

ICT and E-learning – www.niace.org.uk/lifelonglearningenquiry

Minimum Core Standards – http://repository.excellencegateway.org.uk/fedora/objects/import-pdf:93/datastreams/PDF/content

Minimum Core – inclusive learning approaches for literacy, language, numeracy and ICT (2007) – http://www.excellencegateway.org.uk/node/12020

UNIT TITLE: Delivering education and training

Assessment grid

Learning Outcomes The learner will:	Assessment Criteria The learner can:	Example evidence
4. Be able to implement the minimum core when delivering inclusive teaching and learning	4.1 Analyse ways in which minimum core elements can be demonstrated when delivering inclusive teaching and learning	A written analysis of ways in which you can demonstrate the different minimum core elements, i.e. literacy, language, numeracy and information and communication technology (ICT), when delivering inclusive teaching and learning. For example: *Literacy:* using schemes of work, teaching and learning plans (session plans), annotating qualification guidance, creating supporting materials for the delivery of your specialist subject. *Language:* giving clear instructions to your learners. *Numeracy:* devising and amending the timing of teaching, learning and assessment activities during a session. *ICT:* using new technology for activities, for example, using voting pods to complete a gapped handout or using digital media for visual/audio recording and playback of activities and presentations.
	4.2 Apply minimum core elements in delivering inclusive teaching and learning	Anonymised evidence of using the different minimum core elements when delivering inclusive teaching and learning such as: *Literacy* • action plans • group profile • handouts • learning materials, for example, word activities • programme rationale • scheme of work • teaching and learning plans (session plans) • tutorial review records • website or VLE content. *Language* • a visual or digital recording of you speaking to your learners and responding to their questions (with their permission) • a visual or digital recording of a session where you have received feedback from your learners regarding how effectively you communicated with them regarding various activities. *Numeracy* • an analysis of the timings of activities carried out by learners during sessions • a statistical analysis of data received from surveys • budgeting for the cost of materials, equipment and resources required throughout the programme • scheduling and timetabling your sessions and the teaching, learning and assessment activities within them. *ICT* • a visual recording of you using technology which you have created/adapted to meet the needs of your learners for activities such as uploading materials to a VLE, communicating and negotiating work activities and agreeing deadlines with learners • appropriate use of social networking, for example, using Twitter to send information to your learners • audio, digital and electronic materials and records you have created and used • emails • online communications, polls and surveys. An anonymised case study demonstrating how you have applied the minimum core elements when delivering inclusive teaching and learning. Your assessor's observation report and feedback, along with records of any discussions.

12 BE ABLE TO EVALUATE OWN PRACTICE IN DELIVERING INCLUSIVE TEACHING AND LEARNING

This chapter is in two parts. The first part: **Self-assessment activities**, contains questions and activities which relate to the fifth learning outcome of the Certificate in Education and Training unit Delivering education and training.

The assessment criteria are shown in boxes and are followed by questions and activities for you to carry out. Ensure your responses are *specific to you*, the *subject* you will teach and the *context* and *environment* in which you will teach. When using a quote, make sure you understand what the quote means and how it will fit within your writing. It could be that you agree with what the author has said and it supports what you are saying, or it could be that you totally disagree with it. If so, explain why you agree or disagree and, if it's the latter, state what you would do differently. You need to write what you think, or what your point of view is, and relate it to your specialist subject.

After completing the activities, check your responses with the second part: **Guidance for evidencing achievement**. This guidance is not intended to give you the answers to questions you may be asked in any formal assessments; however, it will help you focus your responses towards meeting the assessment criteria.

At the end of the chapter is an example of a completed **Assessment grid** which gives ideas for evidence you could provide towards meeting the assessment criteria. Evidence can be cross-referenced between units and assessment criteria if it meets the requirements.

Self-assessment activities

5.1 Review the effectiveness of own practice in meeting the needs of individual learners, taking account of the views of learners and others

Q50 Obtain feedback from your learners and others regarding how you have met the individual needs of your learners.

Q51 Review the effectiveness of your practice based on the feedback you have received.

5.2 Identify areas for improvement in own practice in meeting the individual needs of learners

Q52 What areas have you identified which require improvement in relation to meeting the individual needs of your learners?

Guidance for evidencing achievement

5.1 Review the effectiveness of own practice in meeting the needs of individual learners, taking account of the views of learners and others

Q50 Obtain feedback from your learners and others regarding how you have met the individual needs of your learners.

This is a practical task enabling you to obtain feedback from your learners and others. Feedback from learners can come via written and oral questions, online polls and surveys, questionnaires, comment/feedback forms, good-news stories in newsletters and the local press, social media and any other suitable method you wish to use.

Feedback from others can include oral and written comments from:

- appraisal and review records

- awarding organisation reports

- external inspection reports

- colleagues, managers

- good-news stories, i.e. organisational newsletters, local press, online stories

- internal and external quality assurance feedback

- learner comment/feedback forms

- learning support workers, teaching assistants and volunteers

- mentors, peers

- observation reports, e.g. Ofsted, qualification observers, organisation observers

- online polls

- peer observation reports

- questionnaires

- referral agencies, i.e. Job Centre Plus, National Careers Service

- regional and/or national magazine articles or reports

- self-assessment reports, i.e. those required by funding agencies

- self-evaluation forms

- surveys

- workplace supervisors

and anyone else that has an interest in the way in which you deliver an inclusive learning experience for your learners.

Feedback about the way in which you deliver your programme can be obtained formally via an internal quality assurance process to check that your delivery methods are appropriate, or informally via a peer observation report to help develop aspects of your practice.

You should obtain the feedback in the most appropriate way, which might include using your own methods, or those of the organisation. You could include a statistical analysis of the feedback received, including bar charts, pie charts and/or line graphs.

You could read your organisation's last Ofsted inspection report (if applicable) regarding the use of initial and diagnostic assessment, and how teachers plan their sessions. You could review the strengths and areas for improvement, relate these to your own practice and identify if you need to make any changes as a result.

You should keep evidence of what you have done to show your assessor, who might also observe you with your learners. Be prepared to justify all your decisions.

Evidence could include anonymised completed copies of:

- awarding organisation reports
- external inspection reports, i.e. Ofsted
- good-news stories, i.e. organisational newsletters, local press
- internal and external quality assurer feedback
- learner comment/feedback forms
- online polls
- questionnaires
- regional and/or national magazine articles, or reports which may be online
- self-assessment reports required by funding agencies
- self-evaluation forms
- surveys

Q51 Review the effectiveness of your practice based on the feedback you have received.

Based on the feedback you have received, review the effectiveness of your practice.

For example:

You deliver a wide range of activities throughout your session ensuring that your learners are actively involved in their learning. Your learners have stated that they really enjoy the variety of activities you provide and they feel that they are relevant to their specialist subject. However, you feel that you could revisit their learning preferences to ensure that the activities being delivered meet their individual needs and stretch and challenge them further.

The resources you created are accessed by your learners outside of the classroom environment to develop their capacity for independent learning. Your learners share examples of what work they have done since their last session and your resources have helped them with their revision.

You have reviewed your delivery after being formally observed. The feedback in your observation report states that your learners listened to you talking for 45 minutes without any involvement from them during your session. When delivering your sessions, try and use several short tasks to enable your learners to stay focused. If you do need to use longer tasks, try and break these down into 20 minutes for each, with a chance for a discussion or something different in between. If you teach longer sessions, for example, over an hour, try and include a break to enable your learners to experience a change of scenery, obtain refreshments and visit the toilet if necessary.

You could include a summary of the feedback you have received when you evaluated the delivery process. This could take the form of a self-evaluation section at the end of each teaching and learning session plan, or as a journal or diary (written, visual or audio) in which you note any significant incidents. You could record how you felt about the incident, what you would do differently if it happened again, and relate this to a reflective theorist.

To help you with this approach you could apply Gibbs' model of reflection (1998) (see Figure 12.1). You could cross-reference your response to the unit: Delivering education and training (5.2) if you have met the required criteria.

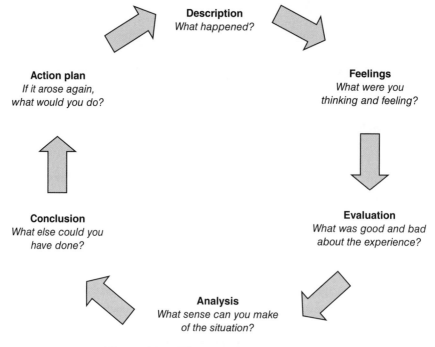

Description
What happened?

Action plan
If it arose again, what would you do?

Feelings
What were you thinking and feeling?

Conclusion
What else could you have done?

Evaluation
What was good and bad about the experience?

Analysis
What sense can you make of the situation?

Figure 12.1 Gibbs' model of reflection

Source: http://www.brookes.ac.uk/services/upgrade/study-skills/reflective-gibbs.html
(accessed 19 November 2013)

Evidence could include documents which relate to delivering sessions, for example, scheme of work, teaching and learning plans, handouts and information sheets, showing how you have reviewed their effectiveness.

> 5.2 Identify areas for improvement in own practice in meeting the individual needs of learners

Q52 What areas have you identified which require improvement in relation to meeting the individual needs of your learners?

This could include the fact that:

You will review the information you obtained from your learners during the initial assessment process to ensure that the range of delivery methods and activities are appropriate to their individual needs. A learner experienced difficulty participating in a practical activity due to a physical disability, which you had not anticipated. This resulted in a significant incident where that learner was not able to complete the activity.

You need to ensure that you keep up to date with new technologies by assessing your own current skills and knowledge. You will explore what is available and discuss possible opportunities with your manager. Learners who are working together on a group project want to set up a group thread on your organisation's virtual learning environment (VLE) and you want to know how to do this. Having this knowledge will build both your confidence and that of your learners in your ability to use new technologies.

You should relate your response to a reflective theory such as Ecclestone who states there is a danger of reflective practice becoming nothing more than a mantra, a comforting and familiar wrap as opposed to a professional tool for exploration *'people might also want – or need – reflection because they seek interest, inspiration, cultural breadth, critical analysis and reasoning, social insight and awareness, challenge and critique, or to create new knowledge'* (1995: 150).

You could create an action plan identifying areas for your own improvement regarding using technology, with realistic target dates.

You could produce an anonymised case study which covers the full process of designing a survey, implementing it, analysing the results, and identifying the areas which are effective, and which need improvement, regarding the delivery process. The survey should take into account the views of your learners and others.

You could cross-reference your response to the unit: Delivering education and training (5.1) if you have met the required criteria.

Theory focus

References and further information

Brookfield, S (1995) *Becoming a Critically Reflective Teacher*. San Francisco, CA: Jossey-Bass.

Ecclestone, K (1995) 'The reflective practitioner: mantra or model for emancipation,' *Studies in the Education of Adults*, 28 (2).

Gravells, A and Simpson, S (2014) *The Certificate in Education and Training*. London: Learning Matters SAGE.

Kolb, D A (1984) *Experiential Learning: Experience as the Source of Learning and Development*. Upper Saddle River, NJ: Prentice-Hall.

Martin, K (1996) 'Critical incidents in teaching and learning,' *Issues of Teaching and Learning*, 2 (8).

Roffey-Barentsen, J and Malthouse, R (2013) *Reflective Practice in Education and Training* (2nd edn). London: Learning Matters SAGE.

Rushton, I and Suter, M (2012) *Reflective Practice for Teaching in Lifelong Learning*. Maidenhead: OU Press.

Schön, D (1983) *The Reflective Practitioner: How Professionals Think in Action*. New York, NY: Basic Books.

Websites

Gibbs Reflective Cycle – http://www.brookes.ac.uk/services/upgrade/study-skills/reflective-gibbs.html

Teaching and learning theories –http://classweb.gmu.edu/ndabbagh/Resources/IDKB/models_theories.htm

Teacher training videos for using ICT – www.teachertrainingvideos.com/latest.html

Theories of learning – www.learningandteaching.info/learning/

Using VLEs – www.ofsted.gov.uk/resources/virtual-learning-environments-e-portfolio

Video email – http://mailvu.com/

UNIT TITLE: Delivering education and training

Assessment grid

Learning Outcomes The learner will:	Assessment Criteria The learner can:	Example evidence
5. Be able to evaluate own practice in delivering inclusive teaching and learning	5.1 Review the effectiveness of own practice in meeting the needs of individual learners, taking account of the views of learners and others	A reflective learning journal or diary (written, video or audio) which reviews the effectiveness of meeting the needs of learners and relates your entries to a model of reflective practice. A written review of the effectiveness of your own practice. For example, revisiting learning preferences and reviewing how well matched they are to your delivery methods and activities. A written review of the effectiveness of your own practice compared to your organisation's last Ofsted report (if applicable). A written review of the effectiveness of your own practice after delivering a session and/or based on feedback from your most recent observed session. Documents which relate to delivering sessions, for example, scheme of work, teaching and learning plans, handouts, information sheets, showing how you have reviewed their effectiveness. Anonymised completed copies of appraisal and review records, awarding organisation reports, internal quality assurer feedback, learner comment/feedback forms, Ofsted reports, online polls, questionnaires, and surveys. Specific comments and feedback received, whether positive or negative. A statistical analysis of the feedback received, including bar charts, pie charts and/or line graphs. Cross-referenced to the unit: Delivering education and training (5.2).
	5.2 Identify areas for improvement in own practice in meeting the individual needs of learners	A written identification of areas which require improvement, relating them to your own delivery practice. For example, assessing your skills and knowledge in relation to new technologies based on requests for support from your learners. An action plan identifying areas for your own improvement, with realistic target dates. An anonymised case study which covers the full process of designing a survey, implementing it, analysing the results, and identifying the areas which are effective, and which need improvement. The case study should relate to the delivery process and take into account the views of learners and others. Cross-referenced to the unit: Delivering education and training (5.1).

13 BE ABLE TO USE TYPES AND METHODS OF ASSESSMENT TO MEET THE NEEDS OF INDIVIDUAL LEARNERS

This chapter is in two parts. The first part: **Self-assessment activities**, contains questions and activities which relate to the first learning outcome of the Certificate in Education and Training unit Assessing learners in education and training.

The assessment criteria are shown in boxes and are followed by questions and activities for you to carry out. Ensure your responses are *specific to you*, the *subject* you will teach and the *context* and *environment* in which you will teach. When using a quote, make sure you understand what the quote means and how it will fit within your writing. It could be that you agree with what the author has said and it supports what you are saying, or it could be that you totally disagree with it. If so, explain why you agree or disagree and, if it's the latter, state what you would do differently. You need to write what you think, or what your point of view is, and relate it to your specialist subject.

After completing the activities, check your responses with the second part: **Guidance for evidencing achievement**. This guidance is not intended to give you the answers to questions you may be asked in any formal assessments; however, it will help you focus your responses towards meeting the assessment criteria.

At the end of the chapter is an example of a completed **Assessment grid** which gives ideas for evidence you could provide towards meeting the assessment criteria. Evidence can be cross-referenced between units and assessment criteria if it meets the requirements.

Self-assessment activities

1.1 Explain the purposes of types of assessment used in education and training

Q53 List at least three types of assessment.

Q54 Explain the purposes of the types of assessment you have listed in Q53.

> 1.2 Analyse the effectiveness of assessment methods in relation to meeting the individual needs of learners

Q55 List at least six assessment methods you could use with your learners.

Q56 Analyse the effectiveness of the six assessment methods you have listed in Q55, and state how they could meet the individual needs of learners.

> 1.3 Use types and methods of assessment to meet the individual needs of learners

Q57 During your sessions, demonstrate the use of types and methods of assessments with your learners, to meet their individual needs.

> 1.4 Use peer and self-assessment to promote learners' personal responsibility in the assessment for, and of, their learning

Q58 During your sessions, demonstrate the use of peer and self-assessment with your learners. Ensure this covers assessment for, and of, learning.

> 1.5 Use questioning and feedback to contribute to the assessment process

Q59 During your sessions, demonstrate the use of questioning and feedback with your learners. Ensure the methods you use contribute to the assessment process.

Guidance for evidencing achievement

1.1 Explain the purposes of types of assessment used in education and training

---

Q53 List at least three types of assessment.

Your response could list some of the following:

- criterion referencing

- diagnostic

- formative

- holistic

- initial

- ipsative

- norm referencing

- summative

Q54 Explain the purposes of the types of assessment you have listed in Q53.

Your response could state that the purpose of assessment is to find out if learning has taken place. Using different types of assessment enables you to ascertain if your learner has gained the required skills, knowledge, understanding and/or attitudes needed at a given point in time, towards their programme of learning. It also provides your learners with an opportunity to demonstrate what progress they have made, what they have learnt and what they still need to do. If you don't plan for and carry out any assessment with your learners, you will not know how well, or what they have learnt. Assessment should not be in isolation from the teaching and learning process. Assessment is a continual activity to ensure progress and learning are taking place. This is then measured against the targets and learning goals which were negotiated with your learners, and documented in their individual learning plan (ILP).

Depending upon the subject you are assessing and any relevant qualification requirements, you might carry out various types of assessment with your learners which could be on a formal or informal basis. Formal assessment means the results will count towards achievement of something, for example, a qualification. Informal assessments help you see how your learners are progressing at a given point.

The purposes of the types of assessment listed in response to Q53 are as follows:

- *Criterion referencing* – this can be used to assess particular aspects which a learner must achieve, towards the outcomes of a programme or qualification. It enables learners to achieve based upon their own merit, as their achievements are not compared to others. All learners therefore have equality of opportunity. The criteria will either be supplied by an awarding organisation, or you may need to write them yourself.

- *Diagnostic assessment* – this can be used to assess a specific topic or subject and level, and builds on initial assessment. Diagnostic assessments are sometimes referred to as skills tests as they assess the skills of a learner towards a particular subject. The results determine what needs to be learnt or assessed in order to progress further. Some types of diagnostic assessments can also identify learners with dyslexia, dyspraxia, dysgraphia, dyscalculia and other learner needs.

- *Formative assessment* – this should take place continually throughout your learners' time with you. This type of assessment is usually carried out informally to review progress, identify any support requirements and inform further development. Simply asking questions and observing actions can help you assess how your learners are progressing. Assessing your learners on a formative basis will enable you to see if they are ready for a summative or final assessment. You could use activities, quizzes and short tasks for learners to carry out which would make the assessment process more interesting, and highlight any areas which need further development. Formative assessment is usually informal, devised by yourself, and often called assessment for learning as it will help prepare learners for formal assessment. During formative assessment it is important that your learners are prepared for the way in which they will be formally assessed. This will ensure they are familiar with the methods to be used.

- *Holistic assessment* – this can be used to assess several aspects of a unit, qualification, programme or job specification at the same time. It should be a more efficient and quicker system as one piece of good-quality evidence provided by the learner, or a carefully planned observation could cover several areas. Holistic assessment enables learners to integrate knowledge and performance, for example, as part of an apprenticeship programme. It should be planned so that the learner knows what they need to demonstrate and/or produce by a certain date. Assessment of a learner's skills, knowledge and understanding can be much more efficient and cost effective if planned correctly, for both the assessor and the learner. Demonstration of a skill often implies the knowledge required to perform that skill; however, the use of questions can be used to confirm understanding.

- *Initial assessment* – this will give you information regarding your learners, for example, any specific learning and assessment requirements or needs they may have, or any further training and support they may require. The process will also ensure learners are on the right programme at the right level. This should take place prior to, or when learners commence. Initial assessment should ascertain a learner's previous skills, knowledge and understanding. Initial assessment can also be carried out during a session, for example, when a new subject is introduced. A quick question – what experience do you have of this, if any? – will soon give you some idea of what your learner already knows or has experience of.

- *Ipsative* – this is a process of self-assessment to recognise development. Learners match their own achievements against a set of standards or their own previous achievements. This is useful for learners to consider their progress and development. However, they do need to work autonomously and be honest with themselves regarding what they have achieved.

- *Norm-referencing* – this can be used to compare the results of learner achievements to each other, for example, setting a pass mark to enable a certain percentage of a group to achieve or not. You would allocate grades according to a quota, for example, the top 20 per cent would achieve an A, the next 20 per cent a B, and so on. Norm-referencing uses the achievement of a group to set the standards for specific grades, or for how many learners will pass or fail. This type of assessment is useful to maintain consistency of results over time; whether the test questions are easy or hard, there will always be those achieving a higher grade or a lower grade.

- *Summative assessment* – this usually occurs at the end of a session, programme, topic, unit or full qualification. Summative assessment is a measure of achievement towards set requirements or criteria rather than focussing on progress. This type of assessment can often be quite stressful to learners, and can sometimes lead to a fail result even though the learner is quite capable under other circumstances. If you are assessing a pro-gramme where the activities are provided for you, for example, examinations or tests, there is often a tendency to teach purely what is required for the learner to achieve a pass. Teaching to pass examinations or tests does not maximise a learner's ability and potential. They might be able to answer the questions just by relying on their mem-ory. This doesn't help them in life and work, as they might not be able to put theory into practice afterwards, or even understand the knowledge they have gained. Knowing something, and understanding it are quite different. Summative assessment is usually for-mal, devised by the awarding organisation which accredits the qualification, and is often called assessment of learning as it counts towards the achievement of something.

You should relate your response to a quote such as: 'Our freedom of choice regarding assess-ment will vary according to context. We often have more freedom of choice over formative assessment (assessment for learning) compared to summative assessment (assessment of learning), although this will depend on the individual course or programme' (Tummons, 2011: 50).

You could produce an anonymised case study regarding the different types of assessment you have used with your learners and why you chose to use them.

> 1.2 Analyse the effectiveness of assessment methods in relation to meeting the individual needs of learners

Q55 List at least six assessment methods you could use with your learners.

Your response could list some of the following:

- assignments
- case studies
- discussions
- essays
- examinations
- gapped handouts
- journals/diaries

- multiple-choice questions

- observations

- peer and self-assessment activities

- projects

- puzzles and crosswords

- questions: oral or written

- tests

Q56 Analyse the effectiveness of the six assessment methods you have listed in Q55, and state how they could meet the individual needs of learners.

You could create a table to analyse the effectiveness of the assessment methods and state how they could meet the individual needs of learners; for example, the first six assessment methods from the previous bullet list:

Assessment method	Effectiveness	Meeting individual needs
Assignments	Consolidates learning. Several aspects of a qualification can be assessed. Some assignments are set by the awarding organisation who will give clear marking criteria.	Ideal for learners who like to progress at their own pace. Learners might be able to add to their work if they don't meet all the requirements first time.
Case studies	Can make topics more realistic. Can be carried out individually or in a group situation.	They can enhance motivation and interest. Builds on the current knowledge and experience of individual learners.
Discussions	All learners can be encouraged to participate. Allows freedom of viewpoints, questions and discussions. Can contribute to meeting assessment criteria. Ideal way to assess aspects which are more difficult to observe, are rare occurrences or take place in restricted or confidential settings. Useful to support observations to check knowledge. Learners can describe how they carry out various activities.	A learner with a visual impairment could discuss responses rather than writing or using a computer to answer questions.

(Continued)

(Continued)

Assessment method	Effectiveness	Meeting individual needs
Essays	Useful for academic subjects. Can check a learner's English skills at specific levels. Enhances a learner's knowledge by using research and reading.	A learner with dyslexia could complete it using a word processor with a spell check facility.
Examinations	Can be open book, or open notes, enabling learners to have books and notes with them.	Ideal for learners who like the challenge of a formal examination and cope well under the circumstances.
Gapped handouts	Informal assessment activity which can be done individually, in pairs or groups.	Ideal for lower-level learners. Can be created at different degrees of difficulty to address differentiation.

You could relate your analysis to a quote such as: *'Check that your learner knows about, and is prepared for, the assessment methods you plan to use. For example, they will need to prepare for a discussion in advance, and will need to know what you will be covering if you are going to question them'* (Read, 2011: 29).

You could produce an anonymised case study regarding the assessment methods you have used with your learners and how they met their individual needs.

> 1.3 Use types and methods of assessment to meet the individual needs of learners

Q57 During your sessions, demonstrate the use of types and methods of assessments with your learners, to meet their individual needs.

This is a practical task enabling you to demonstrate the use of different types and methods of assessment with your learners, to meet their individual needs. You need to ensure that you are being ethical, fair and safe with everything you plan to do.

For example:

- *Ethical* – by ensuring the assessment process is honest and moral, and takes into account confidentiality, integrity, safety and security.

- *Fair* – by ensuring the assessment activities are fit for purpose, at the right level, differentiate for any particular needs, and that planning, decisions and feedback are justifiable.

- *Safe* – by ensuring there is little chance of plagiarism, the work can be confirmed as authentic, confidentiality was taken into account, learning and assessment was not compromised in any way, nor was the learner's experience or potential to achieve. (Safe in this context does not relate to health and safety but to the assessment types and methods used.)

You should keep evidence of what you have used to show your assessor, who might also observe you with your learners. Be prepared to justify all your decisions.

You could make a visual, aural or digital recording of you using assessment activities with your learners; just make sure you obtain the relevant permissions.

Evidence could include anonymised initial assessment records, copies of assignments, questions and tests. Evidence should also show how what you have used has met the individual needs of your learners, such as a change you have made to an assessment activity, with the reasons why. If you change any formal assessment activities, you may need to notify the awarding organisation if the qualification is accredited.

You could cross-reference your response to the unit: Assessing learners in education and training (2.2) if you have met the required criteria.

> 1.4 Use peer and self-assessment to promote learners' personal responsibility in the assessment for, and of, their learning

Q58 During your sessions, demonstrate the use of peer and self-assessment with your learners. Ensure this covers assessment for and of learning.

This is a practical task enabling you to demonstrate the use of peer and self-assessment with your learners. This approach gives your learners responsibility in the assessment for, and of, their learning. Assessment for learning involves finding out a starting point for future learning and assessment. Assessment of learning involves making a decision regarding what has been learnt so far.

Peer-assessment involves a learner assessing another learner's progress. Some examples of peer-assessment activities include:

- assessing each other's work anonymously and giving written or oral feedback
- giving grades and/or written or oral feedback regarding peer presentations and activities
- holding group discussions before collectively agreeing a grade and giving feedback, perhaps regarding a learner's presentation
- suggesting improvements to their peers' work
- producing a written statement of how their peers could improve and/or develop their practice in certain areas

Self-assessment involves a learner assessing their own progress. Some examples of self-assessment activities include:

- awarding a grade for a presentation they have delivered
- suggesting improvements regarding their skills and knowledge
- compiling a written statement of how they could improve their work

Your learners will need to understand fully what needs to be assessed, and how to be fair and objective with their decisions and any feedback given to others. There should be clear criteria for your learners to be able to make a decision, for example, relating it to the assessment criteria of a qualification. You should manage the process carefully as some learners might feel they have achieved more than they actually have.

You should keep evidence of what you have done to show your assessor, who might also observe you with your learners. Be prepared to justify all your decisions.

You could make a visual, aural or digital recording of you using peer and self-assessment activities with your learners; just make sure you obtain the relevant permissions.

Evidence could include the peer and self-assessment activities which were used with your learners, such as those in the previous bulleted lists. You could also write a statement of how the activities promoted your learners' personal responsibility for, and of, their learning. For example, both methods encourage learners to make decisions about what has been learnt so far, therefore taking responsibility for their learning and becoming involved with the assessment process.

1.5 Use questioning and feedback to contribute to the assessment process

---

Q59 During your sessions, demonstrate the use of questioning and feedback with your learners. Ensure the methods you use contribute to the assessment process.

This is a practical task enabling you to demonstrate the use of questioning and feedback with your learners. The questions you use should contribute to the assessment process and records should be maintained.

Assessment should be a regular and continual process; it might not always be formalised, but you should be asking questions whenever you are in contact with your learners.

There are different ways of asking questions such as:

- *Open:* 'How would you…?'
- *Closed:* 'Would you…?'
- *Probing:* 'Why exactly was that?'
- *Prompting:* 'What about…?'
- *Clarifying:* 'Can you go over that again?'
- *Leading:* 'So what you are saying is…'
- *Hypothetical:* 'What would you do if…?'
- *Reflecting:* 'If you could do that again, what would you change?'

It's good practice to give your learners feedback when assessing them informally to help them know what progress they are making. Feedback is a way of helping reassure, boost confidence, encourage and motivate your learners. All learners need to know how they are progressing, and what they have achieved – giving feedback will help them realise this. Feedback can be given formally, i.e. in writing, or informally, i.e. verbally, and should be given at a level which is appropriate for each learner. Feedback can be direct, i.e. to an individual, or indirect, i.e. to a group. It should be more thorough than just a quick comment such as well done. Feedback should be given in a constructive way and include specific facts which relate to progress, achievement or otherwise in order to help your learners develop.

You should keep evidence of what you have done to show your assessor, who might also observe you with your learners. Be prepared to justify all your decisions.

You could make a visual, aural or digital recording of you demonstrating questioning and feedback with your learners; just make sure you obtain the relevant permissions.

Evidence could include records of the questions you have asked, along with your learner's responses, and the feedback you have given.

Theory focus

References and further information

Gravells, A (2014) *Achieving your Assessor and Quality Assurance Units (TAQA)*. London: Learning Matters SAGE.

Gravells, A and Simpson, S (2014) *The Certificate in Education and Training*. London: Learning Matters SAGE.

Read, H (2011) *The Best Assessor's Guide*. Bideford: Read On Publications.

Read, H (2013) *The Best Initial Assessment Guide*. Bideford: Read On Publications.

Tummons, T (2011) *Assessing Learning in the Lifelong Learning Sector*. London: Learning Matters SAGE.

Wilson, L A (2012) *Practical Teaching: A Guide to Assessment and Quality Assurance*. Andover: Cengage Learning.

Websites

Assessment methods in higher education – www.brookes.ac.uk/services/ocsld/resources/methods.html

Assessment tools (literacy, numeracy, ESOL, dyslexia) – www.excellencegateway.org.uk/toolslibrary

Developing assessment feedback – http://escalate.ac.uk/4147

Initial assessment tools – www.toolslibrary.co.uk

UNIT TITLE: Assessing learners in education and training

Assessment grid

Learning Outcomes The learner will:	Assessment Criteria The learner can:	Example evidence
1. Be able to use types and methods of assessment to meet the needs of individual learners	1.1 Explain the purposes of types of assessment used in education and training	An explanation of the reasons for assessment, i.e. to find out if learning has taken place at a given point in time. An explanation of assessment types such as initial, formative and summative. An anonymised case study explaining how different types of assessment have been used with your learners.
	1.2 Analyse the effectiveness of assessment methods in relation to meeting the individual needs of learners	A written analysis of the effectiveness of at least six assessment methods you could use with learners. An explanation of how the methods could meet the individual needs of learners. An anonymised case study analysing how the methods you have used have met the individual needs of your learners.
	1.3 Use types and methods of assessment to meet the individual needs of learners	Evidence of using types and methods of assessment with your learners, for example, anonymised initial assessment records, copies of completed assignments, questions and tests. Evidence of how the methods have met the individual needs of learners, such as a change you have made. A visual, aural or digital recording of you using assessment activities with your learners (with relevant permissions). Your assessor's observation report and feedback, along with records of any discussions. Cross-referenced to the unit: Assessing learners in education and training (2.2).
	1.4 Use peer and self-assessment to promote learners' personal responsibility in the assessment for, and of, their learning	Evidence of using peer and self-assessment with your learners, for example, the activities which were used. A statement of how the activities promoted your learners' personal responsibility for, and of, their learning. A visual, aural or digital recording of you using peer and self-assessment activities with your learners (with relevant permissions). Your assessor's observation report and feedback, along with records of any discussions.
	1.5 Use questioning and feedback to contribute to the assessment process	Evidence of using questioning and feedback with your learners such as records of the questions you have asked, along with your learner's responses, and the feedback you have given. A visual, aural or digital recording of you demonstrating questioning and feedback with your learners (with relevant permissions). Your assessor's observation report and feedback, along with records of any discussions.

14 BE ABLE TO CARRY OUT ASSESSMENTS IN ACCORDANCE WITH INTERNAL AND EXTERNAL REQUIREMENTS

This chapter is in two parts. The first part: **Self-assessment activities**, contains questions and activities which relate to the second learning outcome of the Certificate in Education and Training unit Assessing learners in education and training.

The assessment criteria are shown in boxes and are followed by questions and activities for you to carry out. Ensure your responses are *specific to you*, the *subject* you will teach and the *context* and *environment* in which you will teach. When using a quote, make sure you understand what the quote means and how it will fit within your writing. It could be that you agree with what the author has said and it supports what you are saying, or it could be that you totally disagree with it. If so, explain why you agree or disagree and, if it's the latter, state what you would do differently. You need to write what you think, or what your point of view is, and relate it to your specialist subject.

After completing the activities, check your responses with the second part: **Guidance for evidencing achievement**. This guidance is not intended to give you the answers to questions you may be asked in any formal assessments; however, it will help you focus your responses towards meeting the assessment criteria.

At the end of the chapter is an example of a completed **Assessment grid** which gives ideas for evidence you could provide towards meeting the assessment criteria. Evidence can be cross-referenced between units and assessment criteria if it meets the requirements.

Self-assessment activities

> 2.1 Identify the internal and external assessment requirements and related procedures of learning programmes

Q60 Identify the internal and external requirements and related procedures regarding the assessment of your specialist subject.

> 2.2 Use assessment types and methods to enable learners to produce assessment evidence that is valid, reliable, sufficient, authentic and current

Q61 What do the terms valid, reliable, sufficient, authentic and current mean in relation to learners producing assessment evidence?

Q62 Use assessment types and methods to enable your learners to produce evidence which meets the requirements of the terms stated in Q61.

> 2.3 Conduct assessments in line with internal and external requirements

Q63 Conduct assessment activities with your learners, which meet the internal and external requirements identified in Q60.

> 2.4 Record the outcomes of assessments to meet internal and external requirements

Q64 Record the results and outcomes of the assessment activities you have carried out with your learners, which meet internal and external requirements.

> 2.5 Communicate assessment information to other professionals with an interest in learner achievement

Q65 List at least four other professionals with an interest in your learners' achievement, and state why they have an interest.

Q66 Communicate assessment information with the professionals you have identified in Q65 and keep anonymised records.

Guidance for evidencing achievement

> 2.1 Identify the internal and external assessment requirements and related procedures of learning programmes

Q60 Identify the internal and external requirements and related procedures regarding the assessment of your specialist subject.

Your response should identify the internal and external requirements and related procedures for your specialist subject. You could make a list of these, which might include some of the following:

Internal

- a dress code

- a behaviour code

- an acceptable use of computer equipment policy

- access and fair assessment policy

- appeals procedure

- complaints procedure

- authenticity procedure

- confidentiality of information

- quality assurance policy

- plagiarism procedure

External

- Awarding organisation requirements such as registering and certificating learners within the required timescale

- Control of Substances Hazardous to Health (COSHH) Regulations (2002)

- Copyright, Designs and Patents Act (1988)

- Data Protection Act (1998)

- Equality Act (2010)

- Health and Safety at Work etc. Act (1974)

- Regulatory Arrangements for the Qualifications and Credit Framework (QCF)

You should then explain the key requirements of the ones you have identified as to how they relate to your specialist subject. For example, the internal plagiarism procedure might require you to speak to your learner first before taking your concern further. An awarding organisation requirement would be to ensure learners are registered within a required timeframe.

You should relate your response to a quote such as: '*Confidentiality should be maintained regarding all information you keep ... All external stakeholders such as awarding organisations and funding bodies should be aware of your systems*' (Gravells, 2014: 79).

> 2.2 Use assessment types and methods to enable learners to produce assessment evidence that is valid, reliable, sufficient, authentic and current

Q61 What do the terms valid, reliable, sufficient, authentic and current mean in relation to learners producing assessment evidence?

Your response could give the following meanings, which all focus on learners producing evidence:

- *Valid* – the work is appropriate and relevant towards the subject or qualification being assessed, and is at the required level.

- *Reliable* – the work is consistent across all learners over time.

- *Sufficient* – the work covers all the assessment requirements at the time.

- *Authentic* – the work has been produced solely by the learner.

- *Current* – the work is still relevant at the time of assessment.

You could relate your response to a quote such as: '*Assessment also refers to the process of collecting proof of competence; this is frequently referred to as "evidence". This evidence is generated by undertaking an observation, questioning session, review of products, completion of assignments or another assessment method*' (Wilson, 2012: 44).

Q62 Use assessment types and methods to enable your learners to produce evidence which meets the requirements of the terms stated in Q61.

This is a practical task enabling you to use assessment types and methods which meet the requirements of validity, reliability, sufficiency, authenticity and currency.

You should keep evidence of what you have done to show your assessor, who might also observe you with your learners. Be prepared to justify all your decisions.

Evidence could include copies of assessment activities you have used with your learners, such as assignments, questions and tests.

You could cross-reference your response to the unit: Assessing learners in education and training (1.3) if you have met the required criteria.

> 2.3 Conduct assessments in line with internal and external requirements

Q63 Conduct assessment activities with your learners, which meet the internal and external requirements identified in Q60.

This is a practical task enabling you to conduct and carry out assessment activities with your learners which meet the internal and external requirements as stated in your response to Q60.

You should keep evidence of what you have done to show your assessor, who might also observe you with your learners. Be prepared to justify all your decisions.

Evidence could include copies of the assessment activities you have used, showing how they have met certain internal (organisation) and external (awarding organisation) requirements.

You could produce an anonymised case study regarding the assessment activities you have used with your learners and how they met the internal and external requirements.

You could cross-reference your response to the unit: Assessing learners in education and training (1.3, 2.1, 2.2) if you have met the required criteria.

> 2.4 Record the outcomes of assessments to meet internal and external requirements

Q64 Record the results and outcomes of the assessment activities you have carried out with your learners, which meet internal and external requirements.

This is a practical task enabling you to make a decision and record the results of your learners' achievements. The results should meet the internal and external requirements as stated in your response to Q60.

You should keep evidence of what you have done to show your assessor, who might also observe you with your learners. Be prepared to justify all your decisions.

Evidence could include copies of the work you have assessed, your assessment records showing your decisions, and the feedback given to your learners. All records should meet internal and external requirements, such as the amount of detail to be documented and the templates and forms you have used.

You could cross-reference your response to the unit: Assessing learners in education and training (1.3, 2.1, 2.2, 2.3) if you have met the required criteria.

> 2.5 Communicate assessment information to other professionals with an interest in learner achievement

Q65 List at least four other professionals with an interest in your learners' achievement, and state why they have an interest.

Your list might include some of the following:

- *administration staff* – to register learners with an awarding organisation
- *awarding organisation personnel* – to ensure compliance with their regulations
- *co-tutors* – to provide information on progress
- *finance staff* – to help with funding, grants and loans
- *internal quality assurers* – to ensure the assessment process is fair
- *learning support staff* – to provide support to learners as necessary
- *managers* – to ensure organisational procedures are followed

- *other teachers, trainers and assessors* – to communicate information regarding learner progress

- *safeguarding officers* – to help ensure the well-being of learners

- *support workers* – to provide help and support when needed

- *workplace supervisors* – to provide information regarding progress

- *work placement co-ordinators* – to arrange and monitor suitable work experience placements

Q66 Communicate assessment information with the professionals you have identified in Q65 and keep anonymised records.

This is a practical task enabling you to communicate with the other professionals you have identified in Q65.

You should keep evidence of what you have done to show your assessor, who might also observe you with other professionals. Be prepared to justify all your decisions.

Evidence could include anonymised copies of assessment planning and decision records, emails, notes of telephone calls, letters and other evidence of communication.

Theory focus

References and further information

Gravells, A (2014) *Achieving your Assessor and Quality Assurance Units (TAQA)*. London: Learning Matters SAGE.

Gravells, A and Simpson, S (2014) *The Certificate in Education and Training*. London: Learning Matters SAGE.

Ofqual (2009) *Authenticity – A Guide for Teachers*. Coventry: Ofqual.

Read, H (2011) *The Best Assessor's Guide*. Bideford: Read On Publications.

Read, H (2013) *The Best Initial Assessment Guide*. Bideford: Read On Publications.

Tummons, T (2011) *Assessing Learning in the Lifelong Learning Sector*. London: Learning Matters SAGE.

Wilson, L A (2012) *Practical Teaching: A Guide to Assessment and Quality Assurance*. Andover: Cengage Learning.

Websites

Assessment methods in higher education – www.brookes.ac.uk/services/ocsld/resources/methods.html

Government legislation – www.legislation.gov.uk

Plagiarism – www.plagiarism.org and www.plagiarismadvice.org

UNIT TITLE: Assessing learners in education and training

Assessment grid

Learning Outcomes The learner will:	Assessment Criteria The learner can:	Example evidence
2. Be able to carry out assessments in accordance with internal and external requirements	2.1 Identify the internal and external assessment requirements and related procedures of learning programmes	A list identifying the internal and external requirements and related procedures for your specialist subject. For example, an explanation of the key points relating to internal procedures, such as appeals, assessment, complaints, plagiarism and quality assurance. External requirements, such as the Data Protection Act (1998), the Equality Act (2010), awarding organisation and regulatory requirements such as Ofqual and Ofsted.
	2.2 Use assessment types and methods to enable learners to produce assessment evidence that is valid, reliable, sufficient, authentic and current	An explanation of what the terms valid, reliable, sufficient, authentic and current mean, along with how they relate to the assessment of your specialist subject. Anonymised copies of assessment activities you have used with your learners, such as assignments, questions and tests. Cross referenced to the unit: Assessing learners in education and training (1.3).
	2.3 Conduct assessments in line with internal and external requirements	Anonymised copies of the assessment activities you have used with your learners, showing how they have met certain internal and external requirements. An anonymised case study of how you have conducted assessments in line with internal and external requirements. Cross-referenced to the unit: Assessing learners in education and training (1.3, 2.1, 2.2).
	2.4 Record the outcomes of assessments to meet internal and external requirements	Anonymised copies of the work you have assessed. Anonymised assessment records showing your decisions. Anonymised records of feedback given to your learners. All records should meet internal and external requirements, such as the amount of detail to be recorded and the templates and forms used. Cross-referenced to the unit: Assessing learners in education and training (1.3, 2.1, 2.2, 2.3).
	2.5 Communicate assessment information to other professionals with an interest in learner achievement	A list of other professionals who have an interest in learner achievement, such as administration staff (to register and certificate learners with an awarding organisation), other teachers (to provide information on progress and achievement) and finance staff (to help with funding, grants and loans). Anonymised copies of assessment planning and decision records, emails, notes of telephone calls, letters and other evidence of communication.

15 BE ABLE TO IMPLEMENT THE MINIMUM CORE WHEN ASSESSING LEARNERS

This chapter is in two parts. The first part: **Self-assessment activities**, contains questions and activities which relate to the third learning outcome of the Certificate in Education and Training unit Assessing learners in education and training.

The assessment criteria are shown in boxes and are followed by questions and activities for you to carry out. Ensure your responses are *specific to you*, the *subject* you will teach and the *context* and *environment* in which you will teach. When using a quote, make sure you understand what the quote means and how it will fit within your writing. It could be that you agree with what the author has said and it supports what you are saying, or it could be that you totally disagree with it. If so, explain why you agree or disagree and, if it's the latter, state what you would do differently. You need to write what you think, or what your point of view is, and relate it to your specialist subject.

After completing the activities, check your responses with the second part: **Guidance for evidencing achievement**. This guidance is not intended to give you the answers to questions you may be asked in any formal assessments; however, it will help you focus your responses towards meeting the assessment criteria.

At the end of the chapter is an example of a completed **Assessment grid** which gives ideas for evidence you could provide towards meeting the assessment criteria. Evidence can be cross-referenced between units and assessment criteria if it meets the requirements.

Self-assessment activities

> 3.1 Analyse ways in which minimum core elements can be demonstrated in assessing learners

Q67 Analyse how you can demonstrate minimum core elements when assessing learners.

> 3.2 Apply minimum core elements in assessing learners

Q68 Demonstrate how you can apply the relevant minimum core elements when assessing learners.

Guidance for evidencing achievement

> 3.1 Analyse ways in which minimum core elements can be demonstrated in assessing learners

Q67 Analyse how you can demonstrate minimum core elements when assessing learners.

Your response should analyse how you can demonstrate the different minimum core elements, i.e. literacy, language, numeracy and information and communication technology (ICT), when assessing your learners. For example:

Literacy

Reading and annotating the qualification guidance to ascertain what the assessment requirements are for your subject. Creating assessment activities and materials such as assignments, tests or questions. Checking spelling, grammar, punctuation and sentence construction of all documents created before issuing them to learners.

You should relate your response to a quote such as: 'All communication should be clear, concise, correct, complete and convincing' (Appleyard and Appleyard, 2009: 100).

Language

Speaking to learners about the assessment process and how it will be conducted. Asking questions to check a learner's knowledge and understanding, and listening to their responses. Listening to questions and answering them appropriately.

You should relate your response to a quote such as: *'our voice can convey a larger proportion of our message than the words we use ... the proportion of our message conveyed through body language can be even higher'* (Appleyard and Appleyard, 2009: 71).

Numeracy

Calculating how long various assessment activities will take. Interpreting how long learners are actually taking to carry out an activity, and what time they have left to complete. Evaluating grades, for example, how many achieved a pass, merit or distinction. Analysing retention and achievement rates.

You should relate your response to a quote such as: *'Numeracy provides the opportunity to communicate information clearly and succinctly'* (Peart, 2009: 87).

ICT

Preparing online assessment materials and uploading them to a virtual learning environment (VLE) or other system. Using a word processor or other application to create assessment materials. Using email or social networking to communicate appropriately. Using new technology for assessment activities such as online live observations, polls, surveys and video conferencing. Using digital media for visual/audio recording and playback of assessment activities.

You should relate your response to a quote such as *Because: 'ICT is a set of tools that allow you to undertake tasks and meet your needs, it is also important to consider the nature of the tasks that you would use ICT to fulfil'* (Clarke, 2009: 64).

3.2 Apply minimum core elements in assessing learners

Q68 Demonstrate how you can apply the relevant minimum core elements when assessing learners.

This is a practical task enabling you to use the minimum core elements you have analysed in Q67.

You should keep evidence of what you have done to show your assessor, who might also observe you with your learners. Be prepared to justify all your decisions.

Evidence could include:

Literacy

- action plans
- assessment activities and materials such as assignments, tests and questions
- assessment plans and review records
- assessment tracking sheet showing achievement dates and grades
- feedback records
- formative and summative records
- observation checklists
- observation reports
- performance and knowledge records
- professional discussion records
- progress reports
- records of oral questions and responses
- standardisation records
- tutorial reviews

Language

A visual or digital recording of you speaking to your learners and responding to their questions (with their permission).

Numeracy

- a statistical analysis of data received from surveys
- an analysis of initial and diagnostic test results

- an analysis of retention and achievement rates

- an evaluation of learners' grades

ICT

- a visual recording of you using technology for assessment activities such as uploading materials, communicating, marking and giving feedback online

- audio, digital and electronic materials and records you use

- emails you have sent (anonymised)

- evidence of online communications, polls and surveys

You could produce an anonymised case study of how you have applied the minimum core elements.

Theory focus

References and further information

Appleyard, N and Appleyard, K (2009) *The Minimum Core for Language and Literacy*. London: Learning Matters SAGE.

Clarke, A (2009) *The Minimum Core for Information and Communication Technology*. London: Learning Matters SAGE.

Gravells, A and Simpson, S (2014) *The Certificate in Education and Training*. London: Learning Matters SAGE.

LLUK (2007a) *Addressing Literacy, Language, Numeracy and ICT Needs in Education and Training: Defining the Minimum Core of Teachers' Knowledge, Understanding and Personal Skills*. London: Lifelong Learning UK.

LLUK (2007b) *Literacy, Language, Numeracy and ICT: Inclusive Learning Approaches for all Teachers, Tutors and Trainers in the Learning and Skills Sector*. London: Lifelong Learning UK.

Peart, S (2009) *The Minimum Core for Numeracy*. London: Learning Matters SAGE.

Websites

Approved literacy and numeracy qualifications – http://www.ifl.ac.uk/__data/assets/pdf_file/0006/27753/Level-2-Literacy-and-Numeracy-Skills-_June-2012.pdf

Computer free support – www.onlinebasics.co.uk and http://learn.go-on.co.uk

Digital Unite – http://digitalunite.com/guides

Digital technologies for education and research – www.jisc.ac.uk

English and maths free support – www.move-on.org.uk

Minimum Core Standards – http://repository.excellencegateway.org.uk/fedora/objects/import-pdf:93/datastreams/PDF/content

Minimum Core – inclusive learning approaches for literacy, language, numeracy and ICT (2007) – http://www.excellencegateway.org.uk/node/12020

Weekly technology updates – http://paper.li/teachology

UNIT TITLE: Assessing learners in education and training

Assessment grid

Learning Outcomes The learner will:	Assessment Criteria The learner can:		Example evidence
3. Be able to implement the minimum core when assessing learners	3.1	Analyse ways in which minimum core elements can be demonstrated in assessing learners	A written analysis of how you can demonstrate the different minimum core elements, i.e. literacy, language, numeracy and ICT when assessing your learners. For example: *Literacy:* creating and proofreading assessment activities and materials such as assignments, tests or questions. *Language:* speaking to learners about the assessment process and how it will be conducted. *Numeracy:* evaluating grades and analysing retention and achievement rates. *ICT:* preparing online assessment materials and using new technology for assessment activities such as online live observations and video conferencing.
	3.2	Apply minimum core elements in assessing learners	Anonymised evidence of using the different minimum core elements when assessing your learners, such as: *Literacy* • action plans • assessment activities and materials such as assignments, tests and questions • assessment plans and review records • assessment tracking sheet showing achievement dates and grades • feedback records • formative and summative records • observation checklists • observation reports • performance and knowledge records • professional discussion records • progress reports • records of oral questions and responses • standardisation records • tutorial reviews *Language* A visual or digital recording of you speaking to your learners and responding to their questions (with their permission). *Numeracy* • a statistical analysis of data received from surveys • an analysis of initial and diagnostic test results • an analysis of retention and achievement rates • an evaluation of learners' grades *ICT* • a visual recording of you using technology for assessment activities such as uploading materials, communicating, marking and giving feedback online • audio, digital and electronic materials and records you use • emails you have sent (anonymised) • evidence of online communications, polls and surveys An anonymised case study demonstrating how you have applied the minimum core elements when assessing learners. Your assessor's observation report and feedback, along with records of any discussions.

16 BE ABLE TO EVALUATE OWN ASSESSMENT PRACTICE

This chapter is in two parts. The first part: **Self-assessment activities**, contains questions and activities which relate to the fourth learning outcome of the Certificate in Education and Training unit Assessing learners in education and training.

The assessment criteria are shown in boxes and are followed by questions and activities for you to carry out. Ensure your responses are *specific to you*, the *subject* you will teach and the *context* and *environment* in which you will teach. When using a quote, make sure you understand what the quote means and how it will fit within your writing. It could be that you agree with what the author has said and it supports what you are saying, or it could be that you totally disagree with it. If so, explain why you agree or disagree and, if it's the latter, state what you would do differently. You need to write what you think, or what your point of view is, and relate it to your specialist subject.

After completing the activities, check your responses with the second part: **Guidance for evidencing achievement**. This guidance is not intended to give you the answers to questions you may be asked in any formal assessments; however, it will help you focus your responses towards meeting the assessment criteria.

At the end of the chapter is an example of a completed **Assessment grid** which gives ideas for evidence you could provide towards meeting the assessment criteria. Evidence can be cross-referenced between units and assessment criteria if it meets the requirements.

Self-assessment activities

> 4.1 Review the effectiveness of own assessment practice taking account of the views of learners and others

Q69 Obtain feedback from your learners and others regarding your assessment practice.

Q70 Review the effectiveness of your practice based on the feedback you have received.

> 4.2 Identify areas for improvement in own assessment practice

Q71 Based on the feedback you have received, what areas have you identified which require improvement in relation to your assessment practice?

Guidance for evidencing achievement

4.1 Review the effectiveness of own assessment practice taking account of the views of learners and others

Q69 Obtain feedback from your learners and others regarding your assessment practice.

This is a practical task enabling you to obtain feedback from your learners and others. Feedback from learners can come via written and oral questions, online polls and surveys, questionnaires, comment/feedback forms, good-news stories in newsletters and the local press, social media and any other suitable method you wish to use.

Feedback from others can include verbal and written comments from:

- appraisal and review records
- awarding organisation reports
- external inspection reports
- colleagues, managers
- good-news stories, i.e. organisational newsletters, local press, online stories
- internal and external quality assurance feedback
- learner comment/feedback forms
- learning support workers, teaching assistants and volunteers
- mentors, peers
- observation reports, e.g. Ofsted, qualification observers, organisation observers
- online polls
- peer observation reports
- questionnaires
- referral agencies, i.e. Job Centre Plus, National Careers Service
- regional and/or national magazine articles or reports
- self-assessment reports, i.e. those required by funding agencies
- self-evaluation forms
- surveys
- workplace supervisors

and anyone else that has an interest in the assessment of your learners.

You should obtain the feedback in the most appropriate way, which might include using your own methods, or those of the organisation. You could include a statistical analysis of the feedback received, including bar charts, pie charts and/or line graphs.

You could read your organisation's last Ofsted inspection report (if applicable) regarding the use of initial and diagnostic assessment, and how teachers plan their sessions. You could review the strengths and areas for improvement, relate these to your own practice and identify if you need to make any changes as a result.

You should keep evidence of what you have done to show your assessor, who might also observe you with your learners. Be prepared to justify all your decisions.

Evidence could include anonymised completed copies of:

- awarding organisation reports

- external inspection reports, i.e. Ofsted

- good-news stories, i.e. organisational newsletters, local press

- internal and external quality assurer feedback

- learner comment/feedback forms

- online polls

- questionnaires

- regional and/or national magazine articles, or reports which may be online

- self-assessment reports required by funding agencies

- self-evaluation forms

- surveys

Q70 Review the effectiveness of your practice based on the feedback you have received.

Based on the feedback you have received, review the effectiveness of your practice.

For example:

Your assessment planning is detailed with realistic target dates – all your learners have stated this is due to your taking the time to get to know them as individuals. They also liked the fact that you discussed what they could achieve within a realistic timescale. You feel the assessment planning templates you use ensured you documented all the requirements to make the planning process run smoothly.

Your decision-making is accurate – all learners have stated they are pleased with the decisions you make, as you always explain which criteria they have met, and what they still need to do. You feel your decisions are accurate as you have worked with the qualification for a while now and have standardised your practice with others.

You could produce a statistical analysis of the feedback you have received, perhaps in the form of bar charts, pie charts and/or line graphs. You could also include specific comments you have received, whether positive or negative.

You could include a summary of the feedback you have received when you evaluated the assessment process. This could take the form of a self-evaluation section at the end of each teaching and learning session plan, or as a journal or diary (written, visual or audio) in which you note any significant incidents. You could record how you felt about the incident, what you would do differently if it happened again, and relate this to a reflective theorist.

To help you with this approach, you could refer to Kolb (1984) who proposed a four-stage continuous learning process (see Figure 16.1). His theory suggests that without reflection, people would continue to make mistakes. When you are assessing, you may make mistakes; you should therefore consider why they happened and what you would do differently next time, putting your plans into practice when you have the opportunity.

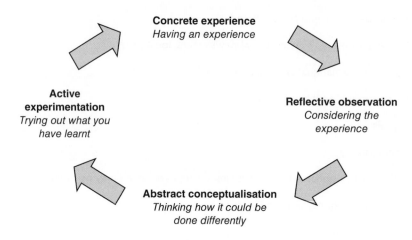

Figure 16.1 Kolb's (1984) four-stage model of learning

This model of learning suggests that the cycle can be started at any stage; that reflection is as important as the experience; and that, once the cycle is started, it should be followed through all the stages for learning to be effective.

You could also review various documents which relate to assessment, for example, initial, diagnostic, formative, summative and holistic, stating how effective they were, what you would change and why.

You could cross-reference your response to the unit: Assessing learners in education and training (4.2) if you have met the required criteria.

4.2 Identify areas for improvement in own assessment practice

Q71 What areas have you identified which require improvement in relation to your assessment practice?

This could include the fact that:

You need to use more technology during the assessment process – some learners have stated they would like to use online assessments to test their knowledge. They feel the paper-based versions you have been using are a bit outdated. You will speak to your manager to find out how you can make this transition.

You need to communicate more quickly with workplace supervisors – you have several learners who are partaking in work experience and some of their supervisors stated they would like to know as soon as their learners achieve a unit of the qualification. You will arrange to meet with them each time you visit the learner's workplace to update them on progress and achievement. You will also email any other relevant information.

You should relate your response to a quote such as: 'While reflecting on yourself, also learn about yourself – think about how you think, how you learn and of the things that interest you; think about your development and potential in such a way that it becomes natural, easy, long term and incremental as you grow in your role as a teaching professional; and think about the impact you are making on your learners' (Rushton and Suter, 2012: 70).

You could create an action plan identifying areas for your own improvement, with realistic target dates.

You could produce an anonymised case study which covers the full process of a survey regarding the assessment process. For example, creating, implementing, analysing the results, and identifying the areas which are effective, and which need improvement. The survey should take into account the views of your learners and others.

You could cross-reference your response to the unit: Assessing learners in education and training (4.1) if you have met the required criteria.

Theory focus

References and further information

Gravells, A and Simpson, S (2014) *The Certificate in Education and Training*. London: Learning Matters SAGE.

Kolb, D A (1984) *Experiential Learning: Experience as the Source for Learning and Development*. Englewood Cliffs, NJ: Prentice-Hall.

Roffey-Barentsen, J and Malthouse, R (2013) *Reflective Practice in Education and Training* (2nd edn). London: Learning Matters SAGE.

Rushton, I and Suter, M (2012) *Reflective Practice for Teaching in Lifelong Learning*. Maidenhead: OU Press.

Website

Online surveys – www.surveymonkey.com

UNIT TITLE: Assessing learners in education and training

Assessment grid

Learning Outcomes The learner will:	Assessment Criteria The learner can:	Example evidence
4. Be able to evaluate own assessment practice	4.1 Review the effectiveness of own assessment practice taking account of the views of learners and others	A reflective learning journal or diary (written, video or audio) which reviews the effectiveness of your assessment practice and relates your entries to a model of reflective practice.
		A written review of the effectiveness of your own practice. For example, revisiting the planning and feedback processes.
		A written review of the effectiveness of your own practice compared to your organisation's last Ofsted report (if applicable).
		A written review of the effectiveness of your own practice after assessing learners, and/or based on feedback from your most recent observed session.
		Documents which relate to assessment, for example, initial, diagnostic, formative, summative and holistic, showing how you have reviewed their effectiveness.
		Anonymised completed copies of appraisal and review records, awarding organisation reports, internal quality assurer feedback, learner comment/feedback forms, online polls, questionnaires and surveys which have contributed towards your review.
		Specific comments and feedback received from others, whether positive or negative.
		A statistical analysis of the feedback received, including bar charts, pie charts and/or line graphs.
		Cross-referenced to the unit: Assessing learners in education and training (4.2).
	4.2 Identify areas for improvement in own assessment practice	A written identification of areas which require improvement, relating them to your own assessment practice, for example, incorporating more technology during the assessment process.
		An action plan identifying areas for your own improvement, with realistic target dates.
		An anonymised case study which covers the full process of designing a survey, implementing it, analysing the results, and identifying the areas which are effective, and which need improvement. The case study should relate to assessing learners and take into account the views of learners and others.
		Cross-referenced to the unit: Assessing learners in education and training (4.1).

17 BE ABLE TO USE RESOURCES IN THE DELIVERY OF INCLUSIVE TEACHING AND LEARNING

This chapter is in two parts. The first part: **Self-assessment activities**, contains questions and activities which relate to the first learning outcome of the Certificate in Education and Training unit Using resources for education and training.

The assessment criteria are shown in boxes and are followed by questions and activities for you to carry out. Ensure your responses are *specific to you*, the *subject* you will teach and the *context* and *environment* in which you will teach. As this unit is at level 4, you should use academic writing and referencing when responding to the questions. When referring to a quote, make sure you understand what the quote means and how it will fit within your writing. It could be that you agree with what the author has said and it supports what you are saying, or it could be that you totally disagree with it. If so, explain why you agree or disagree and, if it's the latter, state what you would do differently. You need to write what you think, or what your point of view is, and relate it to your specialist subject.

After completing the activities, check your responses with the second part: **Guidance for evidencing achievement**. This guidance is not intended to give you the answers to questions you may be asked in any formal assessments; however, it will help you focus your responses towards meeting the assessment criteria.

At the end of the chapter is an example of a completed **Assessment grid** which gives ideas for evidence you could provide towards meeting the assessment criteria. Evidence can be cross-referenced between units and assessment criteria if it meets the requirements.

Self-assessment activities

> 1.1 Analyse the effectiveness of resources used in own area of specialism in relation to meeting the individual needs of learners

Q72 What resources can you use for your subject specialism?

Q73 Analyse the effectiveness of the resources you have identified in your response to Q72, in relation to meeting the individual needs of your learners.

1.2 Use resources to promote equality, value diversity and meet the individual needs of learners

Q74 Why should you promote equality, value diversity and meet the individual needs of your learners?

Q75 During your sessions, use various resources to promote equality, value diversity and meet the individual needs of your learners.

1.3 Adapt resources to meet the individual needs of learners

Q76 Why would you adapt your resources to meet the individual needs of your learners?

Q77 Adapt at least two resources (for example, a handout, a group activity, a presentation, a multiple-choice quiz) to ensure they meet individual needs. Keep evidence of these.

Guidance for evidencing achievement

> 1.1 Analyse the effectiveness of resources used in own area of specialism in relation to meeting the individual needs of learners

Q72 What resources can you use for your subject specialism?

Your response should state the resources you could use for the subject you will teach. Resources are the aids, books, handouts, items of equipment, objects, technology and people that you can use to help deliver and assess your subject.

You could create a table like the following one, in which to list the resources you use.

Information and communication technology	Objects
Audio, visual and digital recorders	Animals
Calculators	Apparatus
Camcorder	Costumes and hats
CD ROMs	Games
Computers/laptops/netbooks/tablets	Models
Digital cameras	Pens, pencils, highlighters, rubbers, rulers
DVDs	Plants
Epidiascope	Puppets
Graphic organisers	Puzzles
Interactive whiteboards	Samples of products
Internet	Specimens of items
Intranet	Sports equipment
Microscope	The real thing
Mobile phones and smart phones	Tools
Personal digital assistants	Toys
Photocopier	**People**
Presentations	Colleagues, teachers, trainers, managers, mentors, technicians, administrative staff, support staff, employers, supervisors
Projectors and data projectors	
Radio	Friends and relatives
Recording devices	Information, guidance and careers staff
Scanners	Learners (past and current)
Social networking	Manufacturers/suppliers
Television	Other professionals: internal/external agency staff, quality assurers, awarding organisation personnel, subject experts and advisors

(Continued)

(Continued)

Information and communication technology	People
Video conferencing	Specialist speakers
Video recorder	Volunteers and teaching assistants
Virtual learning environment (VLE)	Yourself
Voting technology	
Webcam	
Webinars	
Webpages	
External	**Visual aids**
Cinema/theatre/concert	Charts/posters
Conferences	Display board and pins
Events and workshops	Flannel/sticky/magnetic boards
Exhibitions	Flip chart, paper and pens
Field trips	Maps
Jobs fairs	Overhead or slide projector
Lectures	Photographs
Libraries	Presentation equipment
Museums	Sticky notes
Specialist shops	Whiteboard/chalk board
Sports/leisure centres	Year planner, calendar, diary
Other resource materials	
Advertisements	Original documents
Books	Periodicals
Catalogues	Photocopies of documents
Comics	Promotional literature
Handouts	Publicity materials
Information leaflets	Quizzes
Journals	Reports
Magazines	Textbooks
Manuals	Wordsearches/crosswords
Newspapers	Worksheets

You could create a teacher's toolkit, containing various resources which you can carry around with you. The kit could contain pens and paper, plus activities in case you have spare time during a session. This shows your learners you are well organised and have the tools to carry out your job effectively.

The resources you use will depend on your subject and the learning environment, and should link to the different teaching, learning and assessment activities you have planned to use. If you are teaching in the workplace or in a workshop, using genuine objects and materials from the vocational setting can make the learning more relevant and meaningful. This addresses the concept of purposeful learning, i.e. activities with a purpose enabling learners to use a wide range of skills, and to gain real experiences and support. When teaching a skill, a handout or worksheet may not be as useful as the real thing.

Q73 Analyse the effectiveness of the resources you have identified in your response to Q72, in relation to meeting the individual needs of your learners.

Your response should analyse the effectiveness of the resources you have identified in Q72, in relation to meeting the individual needs of your learners.

You should select at least two of your resources and analyse how effective they were at meeting the individual needs of your learners. You should also consider how well they engaged your different groups of learners.

When creating, using, adapting or photocopying handouts and other written materials, you will need to check that you understand the copyright legislation to ensure that you do not breach it. The Copyright Act (1998) covers copying, adapting and distributing materials, including computer programs and materials found via the internet. It may be that you will have to ask the author's permission to use their materials, and they may need to be acknowledged for their work on your resource.

You should relate your response to a quote such as: 'The act of copying or adapting someone else's work is a breach of copyright. Also any adaptation will be legally regarded as a derived work; so if you simply adapt the work of others, it will still be their work, and they have every right to object, (and are also entitled to any money you make from their work)' (www.copyrightservice.co.uk/copyright/copyright_myths; accessed on 25 November 2013).

The best way of finding out if your resources are meeting your learners' needs is to ask them. If a resource you are using is not effective with some of your learners, try changing the experience rather than the resource. You could explain the resource differently or change a group activity to become an individual activity. Wherever possible, try and use resources which involve your learners actively, rather than passively just reading or observing you.

You should always have a clear rationale to justify the resources you have chosen, and then evaluate them after use. Using the who, what, when, where, why and how rationale is a good basis for determining how relevant, purposeful and effective your resource will be in relation to meeting the individual needs of your learners.

It's possible you could have updated or revised many of your resources in the past, either based on feedback, the success (or otherwise) of their use, or to meet any individual learner needs. However, you will need to make sure they are still fresh, professional-looking and current, i.e. reflecting the latest developments regarding your subject and technology.

> 1.2 Use resources to promote equality, value diversity and meet the individual needs of learners

Q74 Why should you promote equality, value diversity and meet the individual needs of your learners?

Your response should state that resources should be accessible and inclusive to all your learners, while enabling them to acquire new skills, knowledge and understanding in a safe way. When using or creating resources, you will need to ensure they promote equality of opportunity, reflect diversity and challenge stereotypes. Your resources should meet the needs of all learners, for example, dyslexia, dyspraxia, a hearing impairment, a visual impairment, a physical or mental disability. The resources you use should be varied and take account of the different needs of your learners as well as the type of programme they are taking. A resource should therefore be relevant to learning, clearly laid out or described, well presented, up to date, adaptable and purposeful.

You should relate your response to a quote such as: 'Well designed resources should enhance perception: by involving more than one sense there is a greater likelihood that the learner will perceive what is intended. For example, the touch and smell of a piece of wood can be more effective than reading about it' (Reece and Walker, 2007: 157).

Q75 During your sessions, use various resources to promote equality, value diversity and meet the individual needs of your learners.

This is a practical task enabling you to use various resources to promote equality, value diversity and meet the individual needs of your learners.

Your resources should be appropriate in terms of level, quality, quantity and content and be relevant to your subject, the methods of delivery and the expected learning. You should select and use resources which centre around the learner and the purpose of learning. If they can also be fun, they will help ensure that learning is interesting and memorable. You could produce a case study regarding the various locations in which you teach and the resources you use for different situations and learners.

You should keep evidence of what you have done to show your assessor, who might also observe you with your learners. Be prepared to justify all your decisions.

Evidence could include resources you have designed, created and used in their various formats.

You could cross-reference your response to the unit Using resources for education and training (1.1 and 1.3) if you have met the required criteria.

1.3 Adapt resources to meet the individual needs of learners

Q76 Why would you adapt your resources to meet the individual needs of your learners?

Your response should state why you need to adapt your resources to meet the individual needs of your learners, for example, their learning preferences or any particular needs. There will be times when the resources you planned to use are not available or not working. Preparing for unforeseen circumstances comes with experience. Whenever you are due to meet your learners, ask yourself: what would I do if something wasn't available or doesn't work? This will hopefully help you plan and prepare effectively.

Wherever possible, your resources should reflect your learners' interests as well as your subject. For example, enabling learners to choose projects that reflect their own interests will help their motivation, progress and achievement. These could include a range of occupational, vocational, community, cultural and/or family interests.

You will need to consider how adaptable your resources can be for use in other contexts with other learners. One size does not fit all, therefore resources will need to be adapted to suit any particular learner needs. Everyone is different, but all your learners deserve to be treated with an equal level of respect and have equal access to all the resources. Be proactive in coping with differences by talking to your learners and finding out exactly what they require, so that their learning is effective from the start of their programme. When you are considering any changes or alterations to resources, you must make sure they are reasonable. You should keep in mind that your organisation has a legal responsibility to comply with the Equality Act (2010).

Whatever resources you use, it's important to ensure they meet the differing needs of your learners. However, you might have to acknowledge your organisation's resource constraints and budgets, and make best use of what is available.

You should relate your response to a quote such as *'Give your learners choices, so they can select the ways of learning they like best. For example, where at one time you might have set an essay to write, now you could encourage them to choose alternatives such as an audio recording, a PowerPoint presentation or a mind map… It helps too if you raise your learners' awareness of how they learn'* (Hill, 2008: 31).

Q77 Adapt at least two resources (for example, a handout, a group activity, a presentation, a multiple-choice quiz) to ensure they meet individual needs. Keep evidence of these.

This is a practical task enabling you to adapt at least two resources to ensure they meet individual needs. You should keep evidence of what you have done to show your assessor, who might also observe you with your learners. Be prepared to justify all your decisions.

You could create a new resource for use with your learners which promotes equality and values diversity. You could then use it, evaluate it and adapt it as required. When deciding what to use, consider the wide range of resources available, try to be creative and imaginative. Don't be afraid of trying something different. However, if it doesn't work as well as you expected, evaluate why and make further changes as appropriate. You could also keep that resource in your toolkit – even if it didn't work with one group of learners, it might be useful in the future. Time invested in creating resources is never wasted.

You could make a visual recording of you adapting various resources (with relevant permissions).

Theory focus

References and further information

Armitage, A, Evershed, J, Hayes, D, Hudson, A, Kent, J, Lawes, S, Poma, S and Renwick, M (2012) *Teaching and Training in Lifelong Learning*. Maidenhead: OU Press.

Becta (2009) *Harnessing Technology Review 2008: The Role of Technology and its Impact on Education*. Coventry: Becta.

Gravells, A and Simpson, S (2012) *Equality and Diversity in the Lifelong Learning Sector* (2nd edn). London: Learning Matters SAGE.

Gravells, A and Simpson, S (2014) *The Certificate in Education and Training.* London: Learning Matters SAGE.

Hill, C (2008) *Teaching with E-learning in the Further Education and Skills Sector* (2nd edn). Exeter: Learning Matters SAGE.

Powell, S and Tummons, J (2011) *Inclusive Practice in the Lifelong Learning Sector.* Exeter: Learning Matters SAGE.

Reece, I and Walker, S (2007) *Teaching, Training and Learning: A Practical Guide* (6th edn). London: Business Education Publishers.

Wallace, S (2011) *Teaching, Tutoring and Training in the Lifelong Learning Sector* (4th edn). London: Learning Matters SAGE.

Websites

Copyright – www.copyrightservice.co.uk

Dyslexia Association – www.dyslexia.uk.net

Gibbs' reflective cycle – http://www.brookes.ac.uk/services/upgrade/study-skills/reflective-gibbs.html

Learning preference questionnaire – www.vark-learn.com

Online free courses in various subjects – www.vision2learn.net

Online games – http://www.npted.org/schools/sandfieldsComp/games/Pages/Game-Downloads.aspx

Online presentations – www.prezi.com

Puzzle software – www.crossword-compiler.com; www.educational-software-directory.net/game/puzzle; http://hotpot.uvic.ca; www.mathsnet.net

Resources Centre – http://www.heacademy.ac.uk/resources

UNIT TITLE: Using resources for education and training
Assessment grid

Learning Outcomes The learner will:	Assessment Criteria The learner can:		Example evidence
1. Be able to use resources in the delivery of inclusive teaching and learning	1.1	Analyse the effectiveness of resources used in own area of specialism in relation to meeting the individual needs of learners	A list of teaching and learning resources you could use for your specialist subject. A list of the contents of your teacher's toolkit which you could carry around with you to sessions. An analysis of the effectiveness of the resources in relation to meeting the individual needs of your learners. An analysis of at least two of your resources and how effective they were with different groups of learners, stating what you would change and why. Your assessor's observation report and feedback, along with records of any discussions.
	1.2	Use resources to promote equality, value diversity and meet the individual needs of learners	An explanation of why it's important to promote equality, value diversity and meet the individual needs of your learners regarding the use of resources. An anonymised case study regarding the various locations in which you teach and the resources you use for different situations and learners. Evidence of resources you have designed, created and used in their various formats. Your assessor's observation report and feedback, along with records of any discussions. Cross-referenced to the unit Using resources for education and training (1.1 and 1.3).
	1.3	Adapt resources to meet the individual needs of learners	An explanation of why you have needed to adapt your resources to meet particular learners' individual needs. Evidence of adaptations you have made to resources to meet individual needs. A visual recording of you adapting various resources (with relevant permissions). Your assessor's observation report and feedback, along with records of any discussions.

This chapter is in two parts. The first part: **Self-assessment activities**, contains questions and activities which relate to the second learning outcome of the Certificate in Education and Training unit Using resources for education and training.

The assessment criteria are shown in boxes and are followed by questions and activities for you to carry out. Ensure your responses are *specific to you*, the *subject* you will teach and the *context* and *environment* in which you will teach. As this unit is at level 4, you should use academic writing and referencing when responding to the questions. When referring to a quote, make sure you understand what the quote means and how it will fit within your writing. It could be that you agree with what the author has said and it supports what you are saying, or it could be that you totally disagree with it. If so, explain why you agree or disagree and, if it's the latter, state what you would do differently. You need to write what you think, or what your point of view is, and relate it to your specialist subject.

After completing the activities, check your responses with the second part: **Guidance for evidencing achievement**. This guidance is not intended to give you the answers to questions you may be asked in any formal assessments; however, it will help you focus your responses towards meeting the assessment criteria.

At the end of the chapter is an example of a completed **Assessment grid** which gives ideas for evidence you could provide towards meeting the assessment criteria. Evidence can be cross-referenced between units and assessment criteria if it meets the requirements.

Self-assessment activities

2.1 Analyse ways in which minimum core elements can be demonstrated when using resources for inclusive teaching and learning

Q78 Analyse how you can demonstrate minimum core elements when using resources for inclusive teaching and learning.

2.2 Apply minimum core elements when using resources for inclusive teaching and learning

Q79 Demonstrate how you can apply the relevant minimum core elements when using resources for inclusive teaching and learning.

Guidance for evidencing achievement

> 2.1 Analyse ways in which minimum core elements can be demonstrated when using resources for inclusive teaching and learning

Q78 Analyse how you can demonstrate minimum core elements when using resources for inclusive teaching and learning.

Your response should analyse how you can demonstrate the different minimum core elements, i.e. literacy, language, numeracy and information and communication technology (ICT), when using resources for inclusive teaching and learning.

For example:

Literacy

Reading books and handouts for your subject. Creating resource materials such as handouts, presentations, activities and quizzes which are well presented. When creating written resources make sure you consider text style, font and presentation. If you were given one handout with a lot of written information in small text, and another with text in a larger more pleasing font with a few pictures, which one would you prefer to read? It would probably be the latter; therefore the same will apply to your learners. Checking spelling, grammar, punctuation and sentence construction of all documents created, before issuing them to learners or uploading them to a virtual learning environment (VLE) or online system. Making simple mistakes with your literacy can set a bad example to your learners as it shows that you have not taken care to proofread your own work.

When designing resources, any individual needs of your learners should be taken into account, for example, dyslexia, a visual impairment, a physical or mental disability. You may need to produce handouts in a larger-sized font, print them on different-coloured paper, or ensure there is plenty of white space surrounding the text (the blank area around the text/pictures).

You should relate your response to a quote such as: 'Writing intended for your learners must be of the highest quality. It is unfortunate if you make an error in an assignment but if you make one when you write for learners you give them an erroneous example to follow. And some will follow because they will believe it to be correct. So it is vital that you proof read everything carefully, checking and double-checking' (Appleyard and Appleyard, 2009: 105).

Language

Speaking to learners about how to use the resources. Asking questions to check a learner's understanding of using the resources, and listening to their responses. Listening to questions and answering them appropriately. Encouraging learners to communicate whilst using resources, for example, using board games, role plays and other resource activities. Involving learners in a discussion about how well a particular resource helped them to achieve the learning outcomes they were aiming for.

You should relate your response to a quote such as: *'Learners who have a good learning experience usually state that this is because of their teacher. Three important things [that] were missing from their learning experience... were:*

- *something to capture their interest*

- *something to provide variety*

- *an appropriate means of communicating knowledge or skills'* (Wallace, 2011: 121).

Numeracy

Calculating how long various resources will take to create and use for more than one level of difficulty and for different learners. Interpreting how long learners are actually taking to use the resources. For example, calculating the level of difficulty of extension activities to challenge more able learners and how long they will take to complete.

Calculating how long it takes to set up resources in different locations and venues. For example, if you have planned to use the internet during your session and you need to collect laptops or tablets to take to the venue. You will also need to return them after your session has finished; therefore you need to plan time to do this.

Working with your learners to be more independent in their learning, and enabling them to access information and materials in their own time. Helping your learners to work out how much of their own time they have to spend on their learning and what the options are for them to schedule this into their everyday lives.

You should relate your response to a quote such as: *'Practical activities related to the learners' experiences and interests, rather than theoretical verbal instruction, are a good way to introduce new numerical language and concepts. For example, learners may be more interested in percentages if they understand how much money they could save in the "everything reduced by 20 per cent" sale at the music store'* (Peart, 2009: 48).

ICT

Preparing resource materials using ICT and uploading them to a virtual learning environment (VLE) or other online system. Using a word processor or other computer program to create resources. Using email or social networking to communicate appropriately with others. Using new technology to prepare resources and then using them during sessions. Using the internet with your learners to support the completion of activities, for example, giving your learners a website link to follow to access an online learning activity such as drag and drop words into boxes to create accurate sentences.

Cyberbullying is a concern that you will need to discuss with your learners regarding their use of ICT as a resource. You should relate your response to a quote such as: *'The following examples are provided to illustrate the type of activity or behaviour, displayed through social media communications, which the University considers to be forms of cyberbullying:*

- *Spreading rumours, lies or malicious gossip*

- *Intimidating or aggressive behaviour*

- *Offensive or threatening comments*

- *Posting comments/photos etc, deliberately mocking an individual with the intention to embarrass or humiliate them'* (http://www.sheffield.ac.uk/hr/az/cyber-bullying; accessed on 25 November 2013)

2.2 Apply minimum core elements when using resources for inclusive teaching and learning

Q79 Demonstrate how you can apply the relevant minimum core elements when using resources for inclusive teaching and learning.

This is a practical task enabling you to use the minimum core elements you have analysed in Q78.

You should keep evidence of what you have done to show your assessor, who might also observe you with your learners. Be prepared to justify all your decisions.

Evidence could include:

Literacy

- handouts
- posters
- presentations
- real resources such as learning materials related to the vocational setting
- a summary of how you adhere to copyright legislation
- website or VLE content
- written statements as to how you would follow your organisation's sustainability policy.

Language

- a video clip of you using resources with your learners (with appropriate permissions)
- details of people you have invited to talk to your learners, for example, authors, politicians and journalists, i.e. experts in their field and an authority on their subject

Numeracy

- a statistical analysis of data received from surveys
- an analysis of the timings of activities carried out by learners (planned and actual)
- budgeting for the cost of resources required throughout the programme
- schedule or timetable regarding time to plan and prepare for resource development and use

ICT

- a visual recording of you using technology which you have created/adapted to meet the needs of your learners for activities such as uploading materials to a VLE, communicating and negotiating work activities and agreeing deadlines with learners
- audio, digital and electronic materials and records you have created and used
- documents you have created using technology such as podcasts and webinars

- evidence of using electronic equipment such as computers, digital cameras, smart phones and tablets

- online communications, polls and surveys

- research regarding cyberbullying and what this means for your group

You could produce an anonymised case study of how you have applied the minimum core elements.

Theory focus

References and further information

Appleyard, N and Appleyard, K (2009) *The Minimum Core for Language and Literacy*. London: Learning Matters SAGE.

Clark, A (2009) *The Minimum Core for Information and Communication Technology*. London: Learning Matters SAGE.

Gravells, A and Simpson, S (2014) *The Certificate in Education and Training*. London: Learning Matters SAGE.

LLUK (2007) *Literacy, Language, Numeracy and ICT: Inclusive Learning Approaches for all Teachers, Tutors and Trainers in the Learning and Skills Sector*. London: Lifelong Learning UK.

LSIS (2007, revised 2013) *Addressing Literacy, Language, Numeracy and ICT Needs in Education and Training: Defining the Minimum Core of Teachers' Knowledge, Understanding and Personal Skills – A Guide for Initial Teacher Education Programmes*. Coventry: LSIS.

Peart, S (2009) *The Minimum Core for Numeracy*. London: Learning Matters SAGE.

Skills for Business (2007) *Inclusive Learning Approaches for Literacy, Language, Numeracy and ICT: Companion Guide to the Minimum Core*. Nottingham: DfES Publications.

Wallace, S (2011) *Teaching, Tutoring and Training in the Lifelong Learning Sector* (4th edn). London: Learning Matters SAGE.

Websites

Approved literacy and numeracy qualifications – http://www.ifl.ac.uk/__data/assets/pdf_file/0006/27753/Level-2-Literacy-and-Numeracy-Skills-_June-2012.pdf

Computer free support – www.onlinebasics.co.uk and http://learn.go-on.co.uk

Copyright – www.copyrightservice.co.uk

Cyberbullying – http://www.sheffield.ac.uk/hr/az/cyber-bullying

Digital Unite – http://digitalunite.com/guides

Digital technologies for education and research – www.jisc.ac.uk

English and maths free support – www.move-on.org.uk

ICT and e-learning – www.niace.org.uk/lifelonglearningenquiry

Minimum Core Standards – http://repository.excellencegateway.org.uk/fedora/objects/import-pdf:93/datastreams/PDF/content

Minimum Core – inclusive learning approaches for literacy, language, numeracy and ICT (2007) – http://www.excellencegateway.org.uk/node/12020

UNIT TITLE: Using resources for education and training

Assessment grid

Learning Outcomes The learner will:	Assessment Criteria The learner can:	Example evidence
2. Be able to implement the minimum core when using resources in the delivery of inclusive teaching and learning	2.1 Analyse ways in which minimum core elements can be demonstrated when using resources for inclusive teaching and learning	A written analysis of ways in which you can demonstrate the different minimum core elements, i.e. literacy, language, numeracy and information and communication technology (ICT), when using resources for education and training. For example: *Literacy:* using a variety of resources, i.e. handouts, presentations, posters, real resources in vocational settings, understanding copyright legislation, website or VLE content. *Language:* deploying passionate and enthusiastic language when using resources to create enthusiasm in your learners and impact on their motivation to learn. Talking with and listening to learners. *Numeracy:* budgeting for the cost of resource materials during your programme. *ICT:* researching ground rules in relation to cyberbullying and discussing the implications for the group via an online forum.
	2.2 Apply minimum core elements when using resources for inclusive teaching and learning	Anonymised evidence of using the different minimum core elements when using resources for inclusive teaching and learning, such as: *Literacy* • handouts • posters • presentations • real resources such as learning materials related to the vocational setting • a summary of how you adhere to copyright legislation • website or VLE content • written statements as to how you would follow your organisation's sustainability policy. *Language* • a video clip of you using resources with your learners (with appropriate permissions) • details of people you have invited to talk to your learners, for example, authors, politicians and journalists, i.e. experts in their field and an authority on their subject *Numeracy* • a statistical analysis of data received from surveys • an analysis of the timings of activities carried out by learners (planned and actual) • budgeting for the cost of resources required throughout the programme • schedule or timetable regarding time to plan and prepare for resource development and use *ICT* • a visual recording of you using technology which you have created/adapted to meet the needs of your learners for activities such as uploading materials to a VLE, communicating and negotiating work activities and agreeing deadlines with learners • audio, digital and electronic materials and records you have created and used • documents you have created using technology such as podcasts and webinars • evidence of using electronic equipment such as computers, digital cameras, smart phones and tablets • online communications, polls and surveys • research regarding cyberbullying and what this means for your group An anonymised case study demonstrating how you have applied the minimum core elements when using resources for inclusive teaching and learning. Your assessor's observation report and feedback, along with records of any discussions.

19 BE ABLE TO EVALUATE OWN USE OF RESOURCES IN THE DELIVERY OF INCLUSIVE TEACHING AND LEARNING

This chapter is in two parts. The first part: **Self-assessment activities**, contains questions and activities which relate to the third learning outcome of the Certificate in Education and Training unit Using resources for education and training.

The assessment criteria are shown in boxes and are followed by questions and activities for you to carry out. Ensure your responses are *specific to you*, the *subject* you will teach and the *context* and *environment* in which you will teach. As this unit is at level 4, you should use academic writing and referencing when responding to the questions. When using a quote, make sure you understand what the quote means and how it will fit within your writing. It could be that you agree with what the author has said and it supports what you are saying, or it could be that you totally disagree with it. If so, explain why you agree or disagree and, if it's the latter, state what you would do differently. You need to write what you think, or what your point of view is, and relate it to your specialist subject.

After completing the activities, check your responses with the second part: **Guidance for evidencing achievement.** This guidance is not intended to give you the answers to questions you may be asked in any formal assessments; however, it will help you focus your responses towards meeting the assessment criteria.

At the end of the chapter is an example of a completed **Assessment grid** which gives ideas for evidence you could provide towards meeting the assessment criteria. Evidence can be cross-referenced between units and assessment criteria if it meets the requirements.

Self-assessment activities

3.1 Review the effectiveness of own practice in using resources to meet the individual needs of learners, taking account of the views of learners and others

Q80 Obtain feedback from your learners and others regarding using resources to ensure you have met the individual needs of your learners.

Q81 Review the effectiveness of your practice based on the feedback you have received.

> 3.2 Identify areas for improvement in own use of resources to meet the individual needs of learners

Q82 What areas have you identified which require improvement in relation to meeting the individual needs of learners when using resources?

Guidance for evidencing achievement

3.1 Review the effectiveness of own practice in using resources to meet the individual needs of learners, taking account of the views of learners and others

Q80 Obtain feedback from your learners and others regarding using resources to ensure you have met the individual needs of your learners.

This is a practical task enabling you to obtain feedback from your learners and others. Feedback from learners can come via written and oral questions, online polls and surveys, questionnaires, comment/feedback forms, good news stories in newsletters and the local press, social media and any other suitable method you wish to use.

Feedback from others can include verbal and written comments from:

- appraisal and review records
- awarding organisation reports
- external inspection reports
- colleagues, managers
- good news stories, i.e. organisational newsletters, local press, online stories
- internal and external quality assurance feedback
- learner comment/feedback forms
- learning support workers, teaching assistants and volunteers
- mentors, peers
- observation reports, e.g. Ofsted, qualification observers, organisation observers
- online polls
- peer observation reports
- questionnaires
- referral agencies, i.e. Job Centre Plus, National Careers Service
- regional and/or national magazine articles or reports
- self-assessment reports, i.e. those required by funding agencies
- self-evaluation forms
- surveys
- workplace supervisors

and anyone else who has an interest in the resources you design, create, use and adapt to meet the individual needs of your learners.

Feedback about the way in which you plan and use your resources can be obtained formally via external quality assurance or inspection reports or informally via meetings with regional colleagues. For example, when a new programme is being introduced in a specialist area there are sometimes opportunities with regional and national experts to work on the development of new resources. This helps save time and money for all organisations with an interest in delivering this programme.

You should obtain the feedback in the most appropriate way, which might include using your own methods, or those of your organisation. You could include a statistical analysis of the feedback received, including bar charts, pie charts and/or line graphs.

You could read your organisation's last Ofsted inspection report (if applicable) regarding the use of initial and diagnostic assessment, and how teachers plan their sessions. You could review the strengths and areas for improvement, relate these to your own practice and identify if you need to make any changes as a result.

You should keep evidence of what you have done to show your assessor, who might also observe you with your learners. Be prepared to justify all your decisions.

Evidence could include anonymised completed copies of:

- awarding organisation reports

- external inspection reports, i.e. Ofsted

- good news stories, i.e. organisational newsletters, local press

- internal and external quality assurer feedback

- learner comment/feedback forms

- online polls

- questionnaires

- regional and/or national magazine articles, or reports which may be online

- self-assessment reports required by funding agencies

- self-evaluation forms

- surveys

Q81 Review the effectiveness of your practice based on the feedback you have received.

Based on the feedback you have received, review the effectiveness of your practice.

For example:

You have adapted a colleague's handout to give to your learners to explain how to access your organisation's online system in their own time. In the first instance, you were confident that, following your adaptations, the handout was fit for purpose for your learners and they would be able to follow the steps involved. However, you found your learners were asking a lot of questions about how it related to their own computer system. You realised that the instructions were written for the systems in your organisation only and were not generic enough to use with other systems.

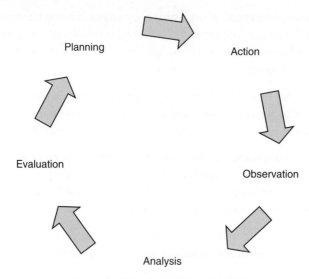

Figure 19.1 The reflective cycle
Griffiths and Tann, 1992

You are teaching in a venue away from the main building, and your learners have given feedback that they feel they do not have access to the same range of resources as learners who are elsewhere. You then decide to discuss this with your manager to ensure all learners can access the same resources.

You could include a summary of the feedback you have received when you evaluated the resources used. This could take the form of a self-evaluation section at the end of each teaching and learning session plan, or as a journal or diary (written, visual or audio) in which you note any significant incidents. You could record how you felt about the incident, what you would do differently if it happened again, and relate this to a reflective theorist.

To help you with this approach, you could refer to Tripp (1993: 54) who stated: 'When something goes wrong, we need to ask what happened and what caused it to happen. The guiding principle is to change the incident into a question. Therefore learners may repeatedly arrive late for a session changes to why do learners repeatedly arrive late to my session? In this way, critical incidents can become major turning points. Asking why enables you to work on the values of your professional practice.'

You could cross-reference your response to the unit: Be able to evaluate own use of resources in the delivery of inclusive teaching and learning (3.2) if you have met the required criteria.

> 3.2 Identify areas for improvement in own use of resources to meet the individual needs of learners

Q82 What areas have you identified which require improvement in relation to meeting the individual needs of learners when using resources?

This could include the fact that:

You asked your learners to write a short paragraph to describe the problems they had accessing the organisation's online system. You could then liaise with your organisation's computer department to ensure that the instructions for access were appropriately written. You admit that you should have practised the steps in your handout in advance of using it with your learners. This would have highlighted the issue before your learners struggled.

You have arranged to go and observe a group which is based in the main building to check what resources are available and which ones the learners are using. You have also arranged with your manager of the venue you are based at to have additional storage space so that more resources can be kept there. You have reviewed the resources you use to evaluate if they can be provided in a different and more accessible format. You have fed back to your learners the actions you have taken so far to resolve this issue.

You should relate your response to a reflective theory such as Griffiths and Tann (1992) who introduced a model of reflection with different timeframes. They state that, without a conscious effort, the most immediate reactions to experiences can overwhelm the opportunity for deeper consideration and learning. They describe their reflective cycle (see Figure 19.1) as having five aspects.

These aspects go through five levels or timeframes:

1. rapid reaction (immediate)

2. repair (short pause for thought)

3. review (time out to reassess, hours or days)

4. research (systematic, focused, weeks/months)

5. retheorise/reformulate (abstract, rigorous, over months/years)

You could create an action plan identifying areas for your own improvement, with realistic target dates.

You could produce an anonymised case study which covers the full process of designing a survey, implementing it, analysing the results, and identifying the areas which are effective and which need improvement, regarding using resources. The survey should take into account the views of your learners and others.

You could cross-reference your response to the unit: Be able to evaluate own use of resources in the delivery of inclusive teaching and learning (3.1) if you have met the required criteria.

Theory focus

References and further information

Brookfield, S (1995) *Becoming a Critically Reflective Teacher*. San Francisco, CA: Jossey-Bass.

Gravells, A and Simpson, S (2014) *The Certificate in Education and Training*. London: Learning Matters SAGE.

Griffiths, M and Tann, S (1992) 'Using reflective practice to link personal and public theories,' *Journal of Education for Teaching*, 18 (1): 69–84.

Powell, S and Tummons, J (2011) *Inclusive Practice in the Lifelong Learning Sector*. London: Learning Matters SAGE.

Roffey-Barentsen, J and Malthouse, R (2013) *Reflective Practice in Education and Training* (2nd edn). London: Learning Matters SAGE.

Rushton, I and Suter, M (2012) *Reflective Practice for Teaching in Lifelong Learning*. Maidenhead: OU Press.

Tripp, D (1993) *Critical Incidents in Teaching: Developing Professional Judgement*. London: Routledge.

Websites

LinkedIn – https://uk.linkedin.com/

Online surveys – www.surveymonkey.com

UNIT TITLE: Using resources for education and training

Assessment grid

Learning Outcomes The learner will:	Assessment Criteria The learner can:	Example evidence
3. Be able to evaluate own use of resources in the delivery of inclusive teaching and learning	3.1 Review the effectiveness of own practice in using resources to meet the individual needs of learners, taking account of the views of learners and others	A reflective learning journal or diary (written, video or audio) which reviews the effectiveness of using resources and relates your entries to a model of reflective practice. A written review of the effectiveness of your own practice. For example, arranging for learners who are in a different venue to have access to the same resources as learners who are elsewhere. A written review of the effectiveness of your own practice compared to your organisation's last Ofsted report (if applicable). A written review of the effectiveness of your own practice after using various resources, and/or based on feedback from your most recent observed session. Documents which relate to using resources, for example, handouts, presentations, social media, showing how you have reviewed their effectiveness. Anonymised completed copies of appraisal and review records, awarding organisation reports, internal quality assurer feedback, learner comment/feedback forms, online polls, questionnaires and surveys which have contributed towards your review. Specific comments and feedback received from others, whether positive or negative. A statistical analysis of the feedback received, including bar charts, pie charts and/or line graphs. Cross-referenced to the unit: Using resources for education and training (3.2).
	3.2 Identify areas for improvement in own use of resources to meet the individual needs of learners	A written identification of areas which require improvement, relating them to your own practice. For example, practising with resources to ensure you can resolve any issues or problems beforehand. An action plan identifying areas for your own improvement, with realistic target dates. An anonymised case study which covers the full process of designing a survey, implementing it, analysing the results, and identifying the areas which are effective and which need improvement. The case study should relate to using resources and take into account the views of learners and others. Cross-referenced to the unit: Using resources for education and training (3.1).

20 TEACHING PRACTICE

Introduction

In this chapter you will learn about:

- teaching practice
- observed practice
- Ofsted criteria and grading characteristics
- the minimum core

Teaching practice

Throughout your time working towards the Level 4 Certificate in Education and Training, you will need to demonstrate that you can put theory into practice by evidencing at least 30 hours of teaching practice. This teaching practice should be in a recognised further and adult education context and with individuals and/or groups of learners. You will be observed for at least three hours at different points throughout your training programme. These observations will focus upon the following three units of the qualification:

- Delivering education and training
- Assessing learners in education and training
- Using resources for education and training

You must use a range of inclusive and differentiated learning techniques and integrate the minimum core throughout your sessions. The minimum core involves you demonstrating your personal skills of literacy, language, numeracy and information and communication technology (ICT). The last section of this chapter explains the minimum core in more detail.

Whilst working towards the Certificate, you should ideally have a mentor, someone who is qualified and experienced in your specialist subject who can give you support and advice. It would be beneficial for you to observe at least one of their sessions and to ask them to observe at least one of your sessions. This process should help you gain new ideas regarding teaching your own subject. You might also like to observe your colleagues or peers who teach different subjects to help you appreciate other ways of how teaching, learning and assessment can take place. Being observed by others before you are formally observed should help you relax a little when the time comes for a formal observation. Any observations by mentors or others will not count towards the three hours of formally observed practice.

You should keep a log of at least 30 hours of your teaching practice activities and cross-reference these to your supporting evidence as in Table 20.1. The evidence you provide should include all the documentation and resources you have used to facilitate your sessions (one piece of evidence can be referred to several times and be numbered), as well as your observer's reports. You should carry out a self-evaluation after each session you have delivered, taking into account your strengths, areas for development, and any actions or improvements required. This might form part of your reflective learning journal or a diary that you are maintaining throughout the programme. Try to be analytical and reflective rather than just being descriptive when you are writing. As you are working at level 4, you should make reference to relevant theories of teaching, learning and assessment.

Table 20.1 Log of teaching practice

Date and time	No. of learners and subject	Location	Length of session	Evidence reference
5th October, 3 pm	15 Level 2 Certificate in Customer Service	Room 7 Main building	2 hours	1. scheme of work (customer service) 2. teaching and learning plan 3. handout 4. self-evaluation form
9th November, 3 pm	15 Level 2 Certificate in Customer Service	Room 7 Main building	2 hours	1. scheme of work (customer service) 5. teaching and learning plan 6. handout 7. copy of presentation 8. self-evaluation form
10th November, 7 pm	12 Level 1 Award in IT User Skills	Room 1 ICT building	1.5 hours	9. scheme of work (IT user skills) 10. teaching and learning plan 11 handout 12. group activity 13. assessment activity 14. self-evaluation form 15. observer's report (one hour)

The evidence you could provide to support your teaching practice includes:

- action plans/individual learning plans

- assessment plans, activities, feedback and decision records

- observer's reports, checklists and feedback

- evidence of integrating the minimum core of literacy, language, numeracy and ICT

- initial assessments

- notes/emails showing liaison and communication with others

- resources such as copies of presentations, handouts, learner activities

- schemes of work

- self-evaluation reports

- teaching and learning plans (session plans)

- virtual learning environments, website pages or other sites and electronic resources you have created or contributed to

- witness statements, i.e. from your mentor

Observed practice

You will be formally observed on at least three occasions, usually for one hour per observation (the minimum being half an hour). You might also be observed on other occasions for any optional units you are taking if this is also a requirement. The results of these observations will count towards achievement of your qualification. In addition to this, you might also be observed by your mentor, a colleague, an internal and/or external quality assurer or inspector. However, the results of these will not usually count towards your qualification. The observations of your teaching practice should be appropriately spaced throughout the whole programme of your learning. You should therefore aim to achieve a good standard of teaching by the end of your programme.

It would be valuable beforehand to see the observation form, the criteria or the checklist that your observer will be using. This way you will have a good idea of what they will be looking for. The feedback you receive afterwards from all of your observed practice should be used to help you reflect upon and develop the teaching, learning and assessment process.

Different observers will be looking for different aspects of the teaching, learning and assessment process. Your observer will be looking to see that you achieve the criteria for the qualification. They might also be observing your progress towards meeting certain Ofsted criteria and grading characteristics for teachers. Ofsted stands for the Office for Standards in Education, Children's Services and Skills and they inspect and regulate services which care for children and young people, and those providing education and skills for learners of all ages. Ofsted state: 'The most important purpose of teaching is to promote learning and improve outcomes for learners' (2012a: 45).

'Outcomes for learners include: achievements that take account of learners' attainment and their rate of progress; progress by different groups of learners; the quality of learners' work; skills development; and progression, including into employment, further or higher education.

Inspectors will consider the main purpose of the particular type of provision when they prioritise the impact that each of the criteria will have on the outcomes for learners' grades.

Criteria

In judging outcomes for learners, inspectors must evaluate the extent to which:

- *all learners achieve and make progress relative to their starting points and learning goals*

- *achievement gaps are narrowing between different groups of learners*

- *learners develop personal, social and employability skills*

- *learners progress to courses leading to higher-level qualifications and into jobs that meet local and national needs.'*

(2012: 42)

If your observer uses the Ofsted grading characteristics, this might result in them giving your session a grade of 1, 2, 3 or 4. Grade 1 is the highest, and grade 4 is the lowest. Alternatively, they might state that your session was outstanding, good, requires improvement or was inadequate (respectively to the 1–4 grades). The feedback you receive should be more important than the grade, as this should help you improve and develop. You should be informed before your observation whether or not it will be graded, and this will depend on the type of observation and who is conducting it. The overall results of teaching observations as part of an official Ofsted inspection report will not grade the quality of teaching, learning and assessment of individuals, only organisations. The Ofsted criteria and grading characteristics are explained in detail later in this chapter.

If your mentor observes you, they should be observing to see how you deliver and assess your specialist subject, to be able to give you relevant advice and support. A colleague may be observing to see that you are following your organisation's quality assurance procedures for teaching, learning and assessment. An external inspector may appear unannounced and might observe you to see if you are giving a quality experience to your learners. An internal quality assurer might observe to satisfy themselves that you are making valid and reliable assessment decisions. An external quality assurer from an awarding organisation might observe you to see that you are following their regulations and assessing accurately. However, all observers will want to satisfy themselves that you are teaching and assessing effectively, as well as supporting your learners towards the achievement of their learning programme or qualification.

Being observed, even if you are an experienced teacher, can be traumatic or stressful, as you will want to deliver a perfect session. However, you are being observed every time you deliver a session by your own learners, it's just that they don't always give you formal feedback afterwards.

If you are nervous, don't let your learners know as they probably won't notice. You are human though and if you make a mistake, your observer will be watching to see that you put it right. Afterwards, they will give you feedback along with helpful advice as to how you could approach things differently in the future.

Preparing for your observation

You should be notified in advance when the observation will take place and how long your observer will stay. You should arrange where to meet them, i.e. at reception or in your teaching area if they are familiar with the venue. Your session might last longer than the time your observer will be present; they might therefore miss the beginning or ending and arrive part way through. If possible, you should try and plan the session to allow time to talk to your observer either before, afterwards or preferably both.

You might want to inform your learners in advance that the session is to be observed, and that it is you being observed, not them. You could state that you expect them to behave in their usual way. Otherwise, they might feel they should be quiet, not ask any questions, or ask too many questions to appear helpful which will give a false impression of what normally occurs. Your observer may want to talk to your learners at some point, and might ask you to leave the room whilst they do this. Don't be concerned, this is quite normal; they like to find out what your learners are experiencing and how your teaching is having an impact upon their learning.

Make sure all the materials you have prepared are of good quality, are varied, address inclusivity and differentiation and are free from spelling, grammar and punctuation errors. Don't try and prepare too much by way of showing off, or use any equipment you are not totally comfortable with. Make sure you have a spare activity in case you have extra time available, and extension activities to stretch and challenge the more able learners. Always have a contingency plan, i.e. hard copies of a presentation in case of an electronic malfunction.

Check the environment and equipment beforehand and complete any health and safety checks or risk assessments. Make sure you have enough of everything for the number of learners you expect, and be prepared by remaining focused and following your teaching and learning plan (session plan). Make sure you have a clear aim with objectives or learning outcomes for your learners to achieve.

Your observer will want to see your documents such as your scheme of work and teaching and learning plan, as well as your resources and assessment materials. They might ask you to give them a copy prior to the session commencing, so that they can refer to them.

During the observation

Your observer will probably arrive early to talk to you beforehand about the observation process, the documentation they will be completing, and arrange when they will give you feedback. They may choose where they want to sit, or you could place a chair in an appropriate place for them where they can see everything.

The session you are delivering may be one of many, for which you will have a scheme of work to follow. You should give a copy of this, along with your teaching and learning plan to your observer. Don't worry if you don't follow your plan exactly – as your session progresses you will naturally adapt the timings and activities to meet the needs of your learners. You might want to give your observer details of your individual learners, perhaps in the form of a group profile, to show how you will be differentiating to meet their needs. Your observer may also want to see your record of attendance/register, and other relevant administrative documents. These might be electronic rather than hard copies, but should still be accessible.

Try not to look at your observer whilst they are with you, they are not part of your group and will not participate in any activities. Don't embarrass them by trying to involve them. They will be making lots of notes throughout the session; therefore try not to be concerned if they don't appear to be watching you all the time, they will still be listening to what's going on. If you can, forget that they are there and ignore them – your learners should be the focus of your session, not your observer.

You could introduce your observer to your learners at the beginning and state they are observing the session, not them as individuals. Having a stranger in the room might lead to some behaviour issues if you haven't forewarned your learners. If so, you must deal with these as soon as they arise and in a professional manner. Just be yourself and, if you are asked a question by a learner to which you don't know the answer, say you will find out afterwards, and then make sure you do.

Your observer might be seeing the very first session of a programme, in which case you will have several administrative duties to perform, including an induction to the programme, ice-breaker and the setting of ground rules. If you are being observed during one of several sessions, you will need to complete the register and include a link to the last session, with time for learner questions or a starter activity at the beginning. Make sure you start promptly, remain in control and are organised and professional with your attitude and manner.

Keep your teaching and learning plan handy; you could highlight key points which you can glance at quickly to make sure you are on track. You may find that you rush things if you are nervous and lose track of the timings in your plan. If so, have a spare activity that you could give your learners to fill in some time. Depending upon the level of your learners you could give them a crossword, a multiple-choice quiz, or they could have a small group discussion regarding the pros and cons of a relevant topic.

Ensure your learners are engaged throughout and that learning is taking place. Ask lots of open questions to different learners, by name, to check their knowledge as the session progresses. You could have a list of your learners' names and tick them off once you have asked a question or involved them at some point. Use a variety of teaching and learning approaches to address all learning preferences, create opportunities for small group work, encourage peer support, and set challenging extension activities for higher level learners. If possible, use new technology to support the learning process. Above all, make sure learning has taken place. If you are not using formal assessment tasks, make sure you use informal activities which will enable your learners to demonstrate the progress they have made during the session.

At the end of your session you will need to link to the next session (if applicable) and set any homework or other activities. Always plan to finish on time otherwise your learners might decide to leave before you have completed. If the room needs to be left tidy, involve your learners in this before the session finishes. You can then talk to your observer after your learners have left, providing time has been arranged for this.

After the observation

Your observer should give you verbal feedback as soon as possible when your learners have left. Ideally, this should be in a quiet area which will enable you to listen and focus upon what they are saying. Hopefully, the feedback you receive will reassure you that you are teaching correctly and that learning is taking place. However, if you receive some negative feedback don't take it personally, your observer has only seen a snapshot of what you are capable of. You might be given a grade for the session, for example, 1, 2, 3 or 4, or pass or refer. If you receive a 3, 4 or refer, you will be given developmental advice and further support to enable you to work towards a higher grade and a pass next time.

Your observer may also ask you some questions about how you felt the session went, and give you feedback from their discussion with your learners (if they spoke to them). You should take the opportunity to ask questions about how you can improve the way learning takes place, or what you could do differently next time. An honest dialogue will prove very useful to your long term development. You might hear some feedback you don't agree with. Your observer will have seen your delivery from a different perspective to yourself, therefore don't argue, but ask them to clarify how they made their judgement. It could be that you thought everything was going well but feedback from your learners to your observer stated otherwise. If you really don't agree with your observer's decision you could appeal. However, observations are a tool to help you improve your teaching and the learner experience, and you should respect the judgement of your observer. Arguing with them will not help the situation. If you do appeal, you will need to have good reasons as to why you disagreed with their decision. A further observation date might be arranged to enable your observer (or an alternative observer) to visit. Always refer to your last observation feedback when preparing for a future observation. Remember that you are on a learning journey, and you won't get everything right first time. Don't be disheartened, teaching is a very rewarding career and everyone has to start somewhere.

You might want to make notes during the feedback process as you will be receiving a lot of information and may forget some comments. You should be given a copy of your observer's report which you must read carefully. It would be useful to refer to this when writing your self-evaluation of how the session went as it might identify some points for your further training and development.

Afterwards, you could discuss the observation process and the feedback you received with your mentor. They might be able to reassure you if you are feeling sensitive afterwards.

Ofsted criteria and grading characteristics

Some awarding organisations are expecting the providers of qualifications to use the Ofsted criteria and grading characteristics when observing trainee teachers' sessions. It might be that your observer will use them; if so, they should inform you in advance and discuss them with you. The criteria identify key elements of teaching, learning and assessment against which inspectors make judgements. The grading characteristics identify key features of practice at different standards in relation to the criteria.

Ofsted criteria

When judging the quality of teaching, learning and assessment, Ofsted inspectors must evaluate the extent to which:

- *learners benefit from high expectations, engagement, care, support and motivation from staff*

- *staff use their skills and expertise to plan and deliver teaching, learning and support to meet each learner's needs*

- *staff initially assess learners' starting points and monitor their progress, set challenging tasks, and build on and extend learning for all learners*

- *learners understand how to improve as a result of frequent, detailed and accurate feedback from staff following assessment of their learning*

- *teaching and learning develop English, mathematics and functional skills, and support the achievement of learning goals and career aims*

- *appropriate and timely information, advice and guidance support learning effectively*

- *equality and diversity are promoted through teaching and learning (Ofsted, 2012c: 45)*

Your observer might refer to the above comments, and/or they might use the grading characteristics (explained below) which result in a grade of 1, 2, 3 or 4 (or outstanding, good, requires improvement and inadequate [respectively]). Your observer should not expect you to achieve a high grade for your session as you are still learning and developing. They will give you feedback which should be aimed at helping your further development. They should also give advice regarding your progress and ways in which you can improve. However, you should aim to achieve a grade 2 (good) by the end of your programme.

If your observer is using the grading characteristics, don't feel pressured to meet them all just yet, it might take you a lot of practice to work towards achieving a grade 1 or grade 2. Don't be demoralised if you achieve a grade lower than you expected, you are going through a learning experience and your observer will give you advice and support to help you improve. You might find it useful to self-assess what progress you are making towards meeting the Ofsted quality of teaching, learning and assessment grading characteristics. However, Ofsted state they are for guidance only and should not be used as a literal checklist.

Ofsted grading characteristics

The following grading characteristics are taken from the Ofsted *Handbook for the Inspection of Further Education and Skills* (2012b: 50–3). You can view it at the shortcut: http://tinyurl.94z7bx8/kjw2ejq

Outstanding (grade 1)
Much teaching, learning and assessment for all age groups and learning programmes is outstanding and rarely less than consistently good. As a result, the very large majority of learners consistently make very good and sustained progress in learning sessions that may take place in a variety of locations, such as the classroom, workplace or wider community.

All staff are highly adept at working with and developing skills and knowledge in learners from different backgrounds. Staff have consistently high expectations of all learners and demonstrate this in a range of learning environments.

Drawing on excellent subject knowledge and/or industry experience, teachers, trainers, assessors and coaches plan astutely and set challenging tasks based on systematic, accurate assessment of learners' prior skills, knowledge and understanding. They use well-judged and often imaginative teaching strategies that, together with sharply focused and timely support and intervention, match individual needs accurately. Consequently, the development of learners' skills, knowledge and understanding is exceptional. Staff generate high levels of enthusiasm for participation in, and commitment to, learning.

Teaching and learning develop high levels of resilience, confidence and independence in learners when they tackle challenging activities. Teachers, trainers, and assessors check learners' understanding effectively throughout learning sessions. Time is used very well and every opportunity is taken to develop crucial skills successfully, including being able to use their literacy and numeracy skills on other courses and at work.

Appropriate and regular coursework contributes very well to learners' progress. High quality learning materials and resources including information and communication technology (ICT) are available and are used by staff and learners during and between learning and assessment sessions.

Marking and constructive feedback from staff are frequent and of a consistent quality, leading to high levels of engagement and interest.

The teaching of English, mathematics and functional skills is consistently good with much outstanding. Teachers and other staff enthuse and motivate most learners to participate in a wide range of learning activities.

Equality and diversity are integrated fully into the learning experience. Staff manage learners' behaviour skilfully; they show great awareness of equality and diversity in teaching sessions.

Advice, guidance and support motivate learners to secure the best possible opportunities for success in their learning and progression.

Good (grade 2)
Teaching, learning and assessment are predominantly good, with examples of outstanding teaching. All staff are able to develop learners' skills and knowledge regardless of their backgrounds. As a result, learners make good progress.

Staff have high expectations of all learners. Staff in most curriculum and learning programme areas use their well-developed skills and expertise to assess learners' prior skills, knowledge and understanding accurately, to plan effectively and set challenging tasks. They use effective teaching, learning and assessment strategies that, together with appropriately targeted support and intervention, match most learners' individual needs effectively.

Teaching generally develops learners' resilience, confidence and independence when tackling challenging activities. Staff listen perceptively to, carefully observe, and skilfully question learners during learning sessions. Teaching deepens learners' knowledge and understanding consistently and promotes the development of independent learning skills. Good use of resources, including ICT, and regular coursework contribute well to learners' progress.

Staff assess learners' progress regularly and accurately and discuss assessments with them so that learners know how well they have done and what they need to do to improve.

The teaching of English, mathematics and functional skills is generally good. Teachers and other staff enthuse and motivate most learners to participate in a wide range of learning activities.

Equality and diversity are promoted and learners' behaviour is managed well, although some work is still needed to integrate aspects of equality and diversity into learning fully.

Advice, guidance and support provide good opportunities for learners to be motivated and make the necessary connection between learning and successful progression.

Requires improvement (grade 3)
Teaching, learning and assessment require improvement and are not yet good. They result in most learners, and groups of learners, making progress that is broadly in line with that made by learners nationally with similar starting points. However, there are weaknesses in areas of delivery, such as in learning or assessment.

There is likely to be some good teaching, learning and assessment and there are no endemic inadequacies in particular courses, across levels or age groups, or for particular groups of learners. Staff work with and develop skills and knowledge in learners from different backgrounds satisfactorily. Staff expectations enable most learners to work hard and achieve satisfactorily, and encourage them to make progress. Due attention is given to the careful initial assessment and ongoing assessment of learners' progress, but these are not always conducted rigorously enough, which may result in some unnecessary repetition of work for learners, and tasks being planned and set that do not fully challenge them.

Staff monitor learners' work during learning sessions, set appropriate tasks and are capable of adjusting their plans to support learning. These adaptations are usually successful but occasionally are not timely or relevant, and this slows learning for some learners.

Teaching strategies ensure that learners' individual needs are usually met. Staff deploy available additional support carefully, use available resources well and set appropriate coursework for learners.

Learners are informed about the progress they are making and how to improve further through marking and dialogue with staff that is usually timely and encouraging. This approach ensures that most learners want to work hard and improve.

The teaching of English, mathematics and functional skills is satisfactory overall.

The promotion of equality and support for diversity in teaching and learning are satisfactory.

Advice, guidance and support help to motivate learners to succeed in their learning and progress.

Inadequate (grade 4)
Teaching, learning and assessment are likely to be inadequate where any of the following apply:

- As a result of weak teaching, learning and assessment over time, learners or groups of learners are making inadequate progress and have been unsuccessful in attaining their learning goals.

- Staff do not have sufficiently high expectations and, over time, teaching fails to excite, enthuse, engage or motivate particular groups of learners, including those with learning difficulties and/or disabilities.

- Staff lack expertise and the ability to promote learning.

- Learning activities and resources are not sufficiently well matched to the needs of learners and, as a result, they make inadequate progress.

- Teaching of English, mathematics and functional skills is inadequate and a significant proportion of learners do not receive appropriate support to address English, mathematics and language needs.

- Learning activities and resources are not sufficiently well matched to the needs of learners and, as a result, they make inadequate progress.

- Staff show insufficient understanding and promote equality and diversity insufficiently in teaching sessions.

The minimum core

All teachers should have a knowledge and understanding of the following four elements:

- literacy

- language

- numeracy

- information and communication technology (ICT)

These are known as the minimum core and are integrated into the four mandatory units of the Certificate which are at level 4. Your observer may be looking for evidence of how you demonstrate your personal skills in these elements when they visit you.

The minimum core aims to:

- *promote an understanding that underpinning literacy, language, numeracy and ICT skills may be needed for learners to succeed and achieve their chosen qualification*

- *encourage the development of inclusive practices to addressing the literacy, language, numeracy and ICT needs of learners*

- *raise awareness of the benefits to learners of developing embedded approaches to teaching, learning and assessment of English, maths and ICT*

- *provide signposts to useful materials which will support collaborative working with specialist teachers of literacy, language, numeracy and ICT in understanding how to integrate these skills within other areas of specialism (LLUK, 2007: 6).*

Developing and improving your personal skills in these areas will enable you to consider how best to teach your subject in ways that also support the development of your learners' own skills. You will need to meet the needs of your learners whose levels of literacy, language, numeracy and ICT skills might otherwise jeopardise or hinder their learning. You therefore need to ensure your own skills and knowledge are adequate, to help improve those of your learners. For example, you might encourage your learners to use the latest online applications, but not feel confident at using them yourself.

The knowledge and understanding required for you to demonstrate your competence in the personal skills should be taught as part of the Certificate programme you are undertaking. The taught aspects are often referred to as Part A, with your personal skills referred to as Part B. This is due to the referencing of the sections of the document they are listed in. Links to the minimum core documents are at the end of the chapter.

If you are not competent or confident with your personal skills, you might be making errors and not know any different. When planning your sessions, consider how you will demonstrate the four skills. Also consider which skills you want your learners to demonstrate, for example, the use of literacy and language when they are writing. When reviewing their work, you can comment on any errors of spelling, grammar and punctuation to help your learners improve.

Part of your role might be to embed the functional skills of English, maths and ICT within your teaching. If so, you will need to enable your learners to demonstrate these skills themselves, which are similar to the skills you will demonstrate as part of the minimum core.

Some examples of demonstrating elements of the minimum core's personal skills during your sessions are:

- *Literacy* – reading, writing, spelling, grammar, punctuation, syntax;

- *Language* – speaking, listening, discussing, role play, interviews;

- *Numeracy* – calculations, interpretations, evaluations, measurements;

- *ICT* – online applications, e-learning programs, word processing, use of an interactive whiteboard and/or virtual learning environment (VLE), writing emails, using video conferencing, podcasts and other aspects of new technology.

You might like to take additional learning programmes yourself, for example, if your computer skills need further development or you feel your spelling and grammar need to be improved. When you are teaching, your learners will trust and believe you. If you spell words incorrectly in a handout or a presentation, your learners will think the spelling is correct because you are their teacher and they expect you to be right.

To evidence the minimum core, you will need to demonstrate your personal skills in the four elements. Your observer will be looking for aspects of these when they visit you.

For example:

Literacy and language

You should have knowledge about language and of the four skills of speaking, listening, reading and writing and be able to show you understand these by putting them into practice. Demonstrating your personal skills will be shown by the way you communicate with your learners (verbal and non-verbal), how you respond to situations, what reference and support materials you use and how your convey your literacy, i.e. using accurate spelling, grammar and punctuation in written text. Evidence you could provide includes your scheme of work, teaching and learning plans, activities you have designed for learners, resource materials, handouts and presentations.

Numeracy

You should have knowledge about numerical communication and processes and be able to show you understand these by putting them into practice. Demonstrating your personal skills will be shown by how you communicate with others regarding numeracy (to support your role and your learners), and how you use processes such as analysing data, making calculations and solving problems. Evidence you could provide includes statistical analyses, reports, retention, achievement and success data and financial calculations.

ICT

You should have knowledge about ICT and processes and be able to show you understand these by putting them into practice. Demonstrating your personal skills will be shown by how you communicate with others in a variety of ways and how you use ICT systems to support teaching, learning and assessment. Evidence you could provide includes practical examples of using ICT such as emails, presentation equipment, software packages, a virtual learning environment (VLE), an interactive whiteboard, the internet, online applications and documents you have produced electronically such as handouts and activities.

You may be able to use recognised qualifications as evidence of the minimum core, for example:

- Key Skills in Communication at level 2 or above

- Ordinary (O) level or GCSE English (A*–C)

- National literacy and numeracy test level 2

- Functional Skills in Maths at level 2 or above

- Ordinary (O) level or GCSE maths (A*–C) or CSE grade 1 maths

You will need to discuss any prior achievements you have with your assessor, to enable them to check whether they are acceptable, or whether you need to demonstrate any personal skills further.

Summary

In this chapter you have learnt about:

- teaching practice

- observed practice

- Ofsted criteria and grading characteristics

- the Minimum Core

Theory focus

References and further information

Duckworth, V, Wood, J, Dickinson, J and Bostock, J (2010) *Successful Teaching Practice in the Lifelong Learning Sector*. London: Learning Matters.

Gravells, A and Simpson, S (2014) *The Certificate in Education and Training*. London: Learning Matters SAGE.

LLUK (2007) *Literacy, Language, Numeracy and ICT: Inclusive Learning Approaches for all Teachers, Tutors and Trainers in the Learning and Skills Sector*. London: Lifelong Learning UK.

LSIS (2007 revised 2013) *Addressing Literacy, Language, Numeracy and ICT Needs in Education and Training: Defining the Minimum Core of Teachers' Knowledge, Understanding and Personal Skills – A Guide for Initial Teacher Education Programmes*. Coventry: Learning and Skills Improvement Service.

LSIS (2013) *Qualification Guidance for Awarding Organisations – Assessed Observations of Practice within Education and Training Suite of Qualifications*. Coventry: Learning and Skills Improvement Service.

Ofsted (2011) *The Framework for the Inspection of Initial Teacher Education 2012*. Manchester: Ofsted.

Ofsted (2012a) *Common Inspection Framework for Further Education and Skills*. Manchester: Ofsted.

Ofsted (2012b) *Handbook for the Inspection of Further Education and Skills*. Manchester: Ofsted.

Ofsted (2012c) *Initial Teacher Education (ITE) Inspection Handbook*. Manchester: Ofsted.

O'leary, M (2013) *Classroom Observation: A Guide to the Effective Observation of Teaching and Learning*. Abingdon: Routledge.

Websites

Ann Gravells – videos to support teaching, learning and assessment – https://www.youtube.com/channel/UCEQQRbP7x4L7NAy4wsQi7jA

Approved literacy and numeracy qualifications – http://www.ifl.ac.uk/__data/assets/pdf_file/0006/27753/Level-2-Literacy-and-Numeracy-Skills-_June-2012.pdf

Awarding organisations – www.ofqual.gov.uk/for-awarding-organisations

Computer free support – www.learnmyway.com

Digital Unite – http://digitalunite.com/guides

English and maths free support – www.move-on.org.uk

Functional skills – http://www2.ofqual.gov.uk/qualifications-assessments/89-articles/238-functional-skills-criteria

Learning preference questionnaire – www.vark-learn.com

Minimum Core – inclusive learning approaches for literacy, language, numeracy and ICT (2007) – http://www.excellencegateway.org.uk/node/12020

Minimum Core Standards – http://repository.excellencegateway.org.uk/fedora/objects/import-pdf:93/datastreams/PDF/content

Observations of teaching and learning – http://www.excellencegateway.org.uk/page.aspx?o=128948

Ofsted (2012) *Handbook for the Inspection of Further Education and Skills* – http://tinyurl.com/94z7bx8

Ofsted – www.ofsted.gov.uk

Qualification structure for the Level 4 Certificate in Education and Training (36 credits)

The Certificate in Education and Training consists of five mandatory units, which total 21 credits. Optional units to the value of 15 credits must be also be achieved.

The first unit of the Certificate is also part of the Level 3 Award in Education and Training. If you have achieved this unit already, you should not have to repeat it.

To achieve the Certificate, a total of 21 credits must be at level 4 (taken from the mandatory and optional units); others can be level 3 or level 5.

Group A 21 credits must be achieved from this group	Understanding roles, responsibilities and relationships in education and training (3 credits at level 3)
	Planning to meet the needs of learners in education and training (3 credits at level 4)
	Delivering education and training (6 credits at level 4)
	Assessing learners in education and training (6 credits at level 4)
	Using resources for education and training (3 credits at level 4)
Group B 15 credits must be achieved from this group	Optional units – to be chosen from those offered by your provider (see table opposite for examples)
	Credit values vary and the units can be at level 3, 4 or 5
	There are rules of combination regarding which units, levels and credit values can be used to make up the qualification

Examples of optional units	Level	Credit value
Assess occupational competence in the work environment	3	6
Assess vocational skills, knowledge and understanding	3	6
Delivering employability skills	4	6
Deliver and prepare resources for learning and development	4	6
Equality and diversity	4	6
Evaluating learning programmes	4	3
Internally assure the quality of assessment	4	6
Preparing for the coaching role	4	3
Understand the principles and practices of internally assuring the quality of assessment	4	6
Working with the 14–19 age range in the learning environment	4	9

INDEX

A

administrative staff 36
Assess occupational competence in the work
   environment 9
Assessing learners in education and training 3
assessment delivery
   professional interests 123–4
   records 123
   requirements 121–2
   terminology 122
assessment evaluation
   improvement areas 134–5
   review 133–4
assessment, types and methods
   individual learner needs 114–15
   learner self-assessment 115–16
   methods 112–13
   peer assessment 115
   purposes 110–12
   questions 116–17
   terminology 123
   types 110–12
assignments 8, 113t
attended programmes 15
Award in Education and Training 3
awarding organisations (AOs) 4
awards 4

B

Basic Key Skills Builder (BKSB) 45
beginning activities 76
behaviour and respect 30–1
book referencing 13
boundaries 37–8
Brookfield, S 68
buddy approach 30

C

case studies 3, 8, 77, 91, 113t
   points of referral 39
Certificate in Education and Training
   assessment activities 8
   assessment criteria 6–7
   assessment methods 7–13
   mandatory units 3–4
   portfolios of evidence 10

Certificate in Education and Training *cont.*
   professional discussions 10–11
   referencing work 13–14
   reflective learning journals 11, 161
   reflective practice. *see* reflective practice
   study skills 14–15
   working towards 5–6
The Certificate in Education and Training
   (Gravells) 1
certificates 4
checklists 8
codes of practice 19, 23
Coffield, F. 54
communication
   benefits and limitations 84–5
   individual learner needs 85
   learning professionals 85–6
   methods 83
   other professionals 124
contact/non-contact time 3
context 2–3
Control of Substances Hazardous to Health
   (COSHH) Regulations 2002 22, 23, 122
Copyright Designs and Patents Act 1988 22,
   23, 122, 141
Credit and Qualifications Framework for Wales
   (CQFW) 4
credit values 4
criterion referencing 110–11
cyberbullying 148–9

D

Data Protection Act 1998 22, 122
designated teachers 5
diagnostic assessment 111 *see also* initial and
   diagnostic assessment
differentiation 77
diplomas 4
discussions 113t
diversity 20, 55, 70, 77, 142
dual professionals 3
dyslexia 25

E

emergency procedures 30
England 4

enrolment 5
environmental awareness 23
environments 3 see also safe and supportive learning
    environments
equality 20, 55, 77, 142
Equality Act 2010 22, 23–4, 122, 143
essays 9, 114t
evidencing achievement, overview 2–3
examinations 114t
experience, describe, analyse, revise (EDAR) 16, 71

F
feedback
    assessment evaluation 132–5
    inclusive practice 55–6
    individual learner needs 102–5
    overview 8, 10
    planning 55–6, 69
    resources evaluation 154–5
    review from 70–1
    sources 69
    teaching practice 165–6
finishing activities 76
Fleming, N 54
Food Hygiene Regulations 2006 22
formative assessment 10, 111

G
Gibbs reflective cycle 104
Gravells, Ann 1
Griffiths, M 157
group profiles 51, 164

H
Handbook for the Inspection of Further Education and
    Skills (Ofsted) 167
handouts 114t
hazardous materials 23, 30
Health and Safety at Work Act 1974 22, 30, 122
Health and Safety (Display Screen Equipment)
    Regulations 1992 22
Health and Safety policy 30
holistic assessment 8, 10, 111

I
icebreakers 76
ICT
    benefits and limitations 90–1
    code of practice 23
    initial and diagnostic assessment 45, 46
    minimum core 9, 60, 61–2, 63
    minimum core resources 148–50
    personal skills 172
    resources 139–40t
in-service teachers 5
inclusive practice delivery
    ICT 90
    specialisms 78
inclusive practice, meaning of 55
inclusive practice planning see planning

individual learner needs see also initial and diagnostic
    assessment
    communication 85
    ICT 92
    identifying 20
    learning professionals 85–6
    points of referral 38–9
    specialisms 77
    teaching and learning plans 52–4
individual learning goals see initial and diagnostic
    assessment
individual learning plans (ILPs) 45–7, 70
initial and diagnostic assessment 111
    individual learning goals 44–6
    methods 45–6
    role of 43–4
    tests 45
    types 45
ipsative assessment 111

K
Knowles, MS 53
Kolb, DA 134

L
language
    initial and diagnostic assessment 45
    minimum core 9, 60, 61, 62
    minimum core resources 147–8
    personal skills 171
learning models 134
learning preferences 15, 54
learning styles 54
learning support staff 36
legislation 19, 22, 51, 122
literacy
    initial and diagnostic assessment 46
    minimum core 9, 60–1, 62
    minimum core resources 147, 149
    personal skills 171

M
managers 37
mandatory units 3
Manual Handling Operation Regulations 1992 22
mentors 5, 160, 163
middle activities 76
minimum core
    aims 170
    teaching practice 170–2
Modular Object-Oriented Dynamic Learning
    Environment (Moodle) 10

N
norm referencing 112
Northern Ireland 4
numeracy
    initial and diagnostic assessment 45, 46
    minimum core 9, 60, 61, 62
    minimum core resources 148, 149

numeracy *cont.*
    personal skills 9, 171

O
observations 9
observed practice 9, 162–6
Ofsted 68, 103
    criteria 166–7
    grading characteristics 163, 167–70
online assessments 10
online report referencing 14
optional units 3

P
peer assessment 115
personal skills 9, 170–1
Petty, G 77
photocopying 23
plagiarism 12
planning
    inclusive practice 55–6
    personal skills 170–1
    from planning 71
    review 70–1
    teaching practice 163–4
Planning to meet the needs of learners in education
    and training 3
portfolios of evidence 10
professional discussions 10–11
    communication 82, 85–6
professionalism
projects 11
providers 5

Q
Qualifications and Credit Framework (QCF) 4–5
quality assurance 6, 36, 56, 70, 163
questions 11
quotes 13–14

R
referencing work 12–14
reflection model 104
reflective practice
    critical lenses 68
    EDAR 16, 71
    journals 11, 161
    methods 16–17, 71
    reflective cycle *156*
    theories of 157
regulations 19, 22
Regulatory Arrangements for the Qualifications and
    Credit Framework (QCF) 122
resources *see also* minimum core resources;
    resources evaluation
    effectiveness 141
    individual learner needs 141–3
resources evaluation
    improvement areas 156–7
    review 155–6

respect 30–1
rights 55
roles and responsibilities 3, 4

S
Safeguarding Vulnerable Groups Act 2006 22
schemes of work 49–50, 51–6, 164
Schön, D 16, 71
Scotland 4
Scottish Credit and Qualifications Framework
    (SCQF) 4
self-assessment overview 2–3
self-evaluation and action plan 12
session plans *see* teaching and learning plans
Simpson, Susan 1
SMART 70
specialisms
    communication 81–4
    inclusive practice 74–7
    resources 137–41
    technology 89–91
study skills 15
summative assessment 10, 112
sustainability 23

T
Tann, S 157
Teaching and learning approaches 76
teaching and learning plans 52–5, 70–1,
    164, 165
teaching assistants 70–1
teaching, learning and assessment cycle *44*
teaching practice
    log 161t
    minimum core 170–2
    observations of colleagues 160–1
    observed practice 9, 162–6
    overview 5, 160–2
    planning 163–4
technology *see* ICT
timekeeping 23
Tripp, D 156

U
understanding roles, responsibilities and relationships
    in education and training *see* roles and
    responsibilities

V
VARK 54
verbs 6–7t
virtual learning environment (VLE) 10
visual aids 140t

W
Wales 4
website referencing 14
who, what, when, where, why, how (WWWWWH) 16
worksheets 12
written tasks 12